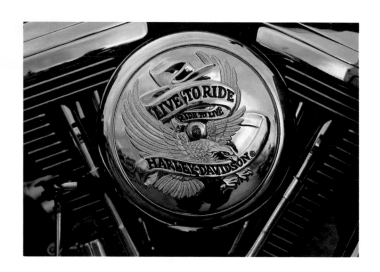

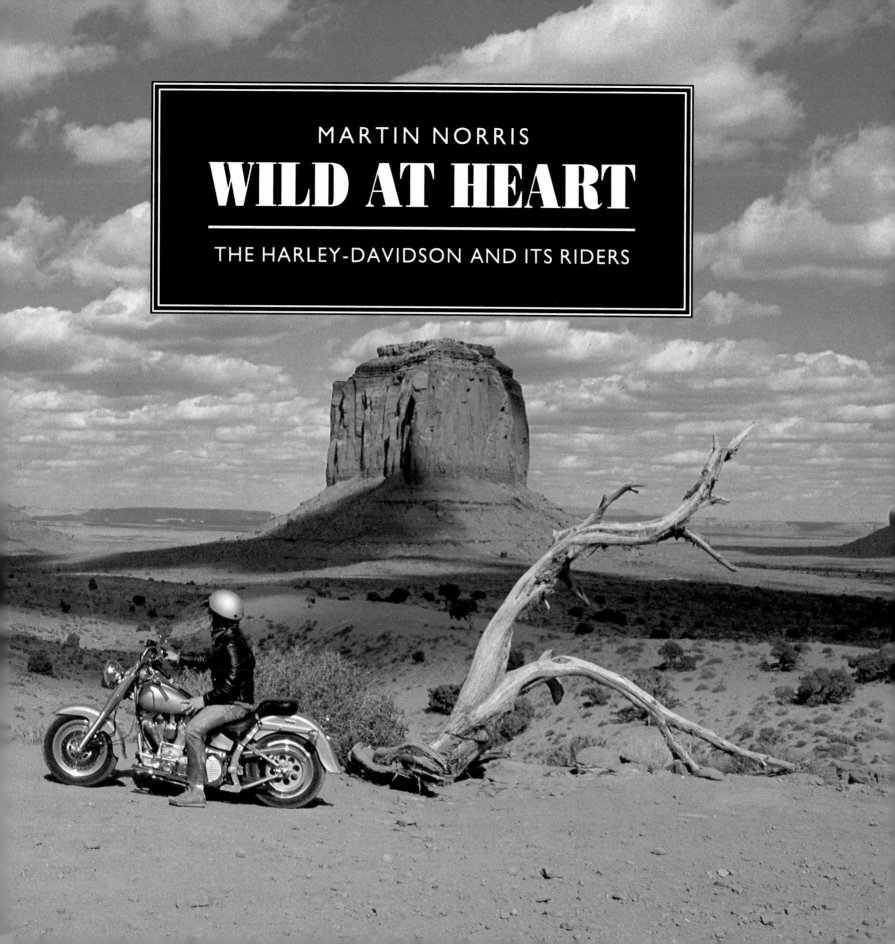

MARTIN NORRIS
WILD AT HEART

THE HARLEY-DAVIDSON AND ITS RIDERS

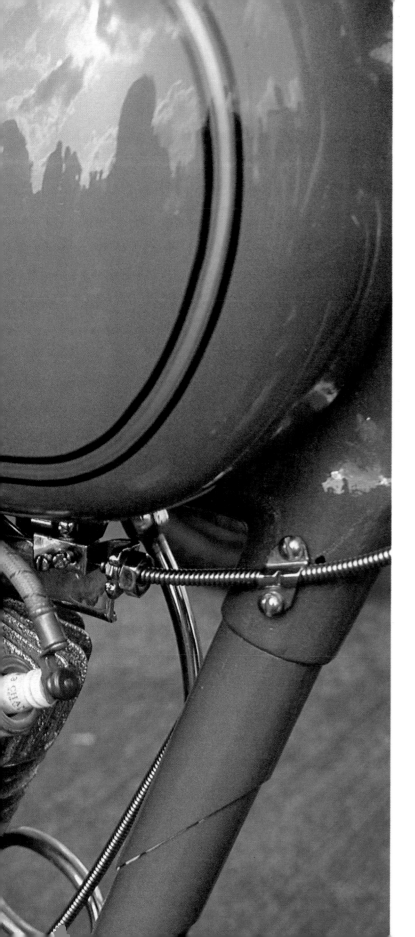

CONTENTS

INTRODUCTION

The Harley-Davidson has a quality about it that appeals to those who have no wish to pass through life insulated and cosseted by the pressure to conform. They have, rather, chosen to be out there, experiencing life the way that they want to live it, aboard a motor cycle that is not anonymous and blandly functional, but which possesses an unrivalled presence and style, as equally uncompromising as its riders.

There are stories that claim that one of William S. Harley and Arthur Davidson's first experiments with the new internal combustion engine at the beginning of the century was to fit a propeller to one of their prototypes and attach it to a rowing boat.

If that was true and they had pursued this project, a part of modern American history would today be missing. Fortunately for us, they turned their attentions to motor-powered bicycles and were later joined by Arthur's two brothers, Walter and William A. Davidson.

The company's early years saw them promoting the reliability and respectability of their motor cycle and the thousands that were purchased by mail delivery companies, armies and police forces reinforced this image. In time, the price of new motor cars dropped, as mass production enabled them to undercut the cost of a motor cycle and side-car. For the man who had money in his pocket and the desire to get from A to B, there was no contest, and motor cycles were generally relegated to the role of utility vehicles or as transport for the poorly paid. Individuals who persisted in riding them out of choice soon came to be regarded as outsiders, in some way, by the many who believe that progress and conformity are mutually esteemed values.

Such an image still endures. But far from deterring people from taking to two wheels it is now encouraging them. In an age where personal transport is becoming increasingly bland and the vehicles less distinguishable from each other, the Harley-Davidson stands alone as the last real motor cycle made today.

Harley-Davidson riders are drawn from every walk of life: from one of the richest men in America who carried around some of his Harleys on his yachts and private jet to a rider from behind the 'iron curtain' who saved for years and sold all of his possessions to realize his dream; from a royal raja in Malaysia who leads his own cavalcades to a lady in America who once broke the transcontinental record and has gone on to ride over a million miles. There is nothing else in the world that could draw together such a variety of people and yet make who they are such an irrelevance.

There is also no event anywhere else in the world like the bike weeks at Daytona and Sturgis that can bring them together as equals. Here amongst the tens of thousands of Harley riders, you might find all of these people sitting around the same table in a bar. They might have all arrived on different types of Harleys, but just as the riders have made their own choice to live and ride the way they want to, so they recognize and celebrate this in others.

Away from the large events there are innumerable clubs that bring like-minded riders together during the rest of the year. Some, like the Vietnam Veterans or the Motor Maids, understandably have certain restrictions about who can join. Others, like the many national clubs around the world or the Harley Owners Group, are open to all.

That a motor cycle can be so many different things to such a variety of people becomes more apparent at a major gathering. Even though the Harley-Davidson is, mechanically, one of the most durable motor cycles ever made and such a large number have been produced over the years, it may come as an initial surprise to see just how many old ones are still in regular use. Such durability is also an encouragement to personalize the machine and everyone adapts and customizes their motor cycle with the assurance that it will still be serving their needs in ten years' and 100,000 miles' time. Others have taken personalization to its creative extreme and built complete motor cycles around the Harley-Davidson engine, elevating customizing into an art form.

Ninety years down the road it is not only the motor cycle that has carried the company this far, but the people who ride them and who have played a major part in making the Harley-Davidson what it is today. Not just another product in the shop, but an enduring symbol of style, individuality and freedom.

MARTIN NORRIS

THE STURGIS AND DAYTONA BIKE WEEKS

These bike weeks have much in common with each other but separated by 2000 miles and six months apart they have their own unique appeal.

The Daytona Bike Week held at the beach resort is geared for entertaining visitors, and consequently has such a full programme of events on offer that visitors can spend all their time going from one to another. Sturgis, though, is a lot more laid back and has the feeling about it of just happening as it goes along.

There are other smaller gatherings at Bowling Green and Laconia that also attract Harley-Davidson riders in their tens of thousands. But the sense of history, location and time of year when Daytona and Sturgis are held combine to create an occasion which makes a visit almost compulsory for Americans, and a lifetime's ambition for motor cyclists around the world.

DAYTONA

Daytona Beach in Florida has been attracting motor cyclists since the dawn of the twentieth century when engines were first being bolted into bicycle frames. With mile after mile of flat sands and a consistently warm climate it was the ideal environment for testing the speed capabilities of motor cycles. Glen H. Curtiss was one of the earliest men to test a machine's capabilities here. In 1904, aboard one of his twin-cylindered bikes, he set a speed record of 67.3 m.p.h. over a ten-mile stretch of the beach. Three years later, astride an experimental V8 aircraft engine that he designed, he made a test run along a timed one-mile section and achieved an average speed of 136.3 m.p.h. Unfortunately he could not establish an official record, for his subsequent attempts with official timekeepers present ended when the frame buckled and a universal joint on the shaft drive broke at speed. In 1912 he turned his pioneering talents to the equally new and exciting world of aviation and the Curtiss motor cycle passed into history.

It was thirty years before this unofficial record could be matched and it took a Harley-Davidson to do it. Joe Petrali, the most successful rider in American racing history, took time out from his competition schedule in 1937 to pilot a highly tuned version of the new Knucklehead to an American record of 136.183 m.p.h. The record was duly inscribed into the history books and the fastest American motor cycle was then retired to the company's motor-cycle museum where it still remains on display. Soon afterwards Joe also gave up motor cycling for flying and eventually became a flight engineer for Howard Hughes.

Above **A much-travelled Main Street character, with a lifetime's memories of rally pins on his chest from all the events he has attended.**

Left **Cruisin' along Daytona Beach while the sun sets and the waves gently roll on to the sand. Can there be any finer experience?**

Above **Vintage racing bikes for sale at the Swap Meet. The bike in the foreground has a short padded bar attached to the petrol tank, which the rider would brace his hip against and push on to help swing the bike sideways to slide around the turns on the oval dirt tracks.**

Right **Bizarre creations are not just restricted to motor cycles here. Isabel Garrett models one of her 'body webs' that she sells to the riders at Daytona. 'It's for the woman who wants to look sexy but not sleazy.'**

By 1935 the speeds that were being achieved by cars and motor cycles along the thin strip of sand were exceeding the limits of the conditions. After Malcolm Campbell piloted his *Bluebird* car through the timing lights at 330 m.p.h. the speed merchants migrated to the infinitely wider Bonneville salt flats.

For a while it looked as if Daytona would slip back into being a quiet holiday and retirement resort again.

The city was faced with a great loss of income if the public stopped visiting the city to watch motor sports, so they organized an annual 200-mile race along the beach. The 3.2-mile oval course that they laid out was unique in racing history. There was a long straight down the beach with a sandy 180-degree turn at the end that sent the rider back down a notoriously bumpy tarmac road, before another 180-degree turn brought him round on to the sand again. When 12,000 people turned up for the first 200-mile race on 24 January 1937 to watch Ed Krutz beat 97 other riders aboard his Indian Sport Scout, the Daytona Bike Week was born.

Racing continued here every year with only a brief interruption during the war years and a move a few miles further down the beach in 1948. By 1960 the bikes had outgrown the circuit as their lap speeds approached 100 m.p.h., and problems controlling the large crowds who were now attending contributed to the event moving to a new home. The last '200' race held on the beach saw Harley-Davidsons ending it in style, taking the first fourteen places.

With the move to the purpose-built International Speedway a few miles inland in 1961, the focus of the Bike Week slowly began to change. The new speedway was a superb and dramatic track with a high banked outer course running round the edge of the arena and with more challenging circuits inside its massive infield. It afforded perfect views for the 35,000 spectators who packed the grandstands, but they were increasingly watching the Harleys losing. Firstly to the British and then to the Japanese motor cycles, whose riders still dominate the winners' rostrum today. After a KRTT Harley-Davidson ridden by Cal Rayborn swept past the chequered flag in

1969, the American motor cycles' precarious dominance of racing ended. It was the last Harley-Davidson to win the Daytona 200.

Today the races are not the reason that many of the Harley-Davidson enthusiasts travel south in March, even though there are supporting races for Classic and 883 cc Sportsters that once again fill the arena with the glorious sound of a V-twin winding the power on down the straight. Much of the action visitors seek today is to be found in the city, along the sand and in the bars. The focus of the Bike Week is now firmly centred on Main Street.

Thousands of bikes are parked along both sides of the street in two lines that seem to stretch to infinity. In between the packed rows

Above left **There is nowhere else in the world where you can sit by the side of the road and see scenes like this. Not only can you ride your Harley on to the beach – but you can also bring the beach to the street.**

Above **The only stock bikes that are seen on the streets of Daytona are vintage restorations. Everyone who buys a new Harley personalizes it in some way to match their personality and, in some cases, to complement their clothes. This duo was competing in the Stock Custom Class at the Rats Hole Show.**

13

Above **A 21 cu. in single cylinder Harley-Davidson (looks like a 1926 model!) on offer at the Volusia Swap Meet. 'For Sale $1850 – Ideal for Restoration'!!**

of sparkling chrome that dazzle in the Florida sunshine, riders slowly cruise along in an endless parade. Park your bike in the middle of this heaving mass and just sit back and enjoy the show. If you wait here for long enough, sooner or later everything on two wheels that you can imagine will ride past – whether it's an amazonian woman in a fluorescent bikini riding a chopper or a 1920s FD piloted by an old-timer of similar vintage. They'll maybe even flash you a smile as they go by.

This is a truly democratic gathering and appearances can be deceptive. The rider that pulls up next to you at the stop sign may look the same as you, but underneath could be a doctor from Denver, an outlaw from Ohio or a housewife from Houston. Some may have jeans that are carefully torn rather than worn through with age, but otherwise the riders, while all individuals, are indistinguishable from each other in spirit.

Despite the intimidating appearance of many of the riders, you would have to search hard to find a friendlier crowd of people. The bear of a man whose beer you have accidentally spilt will invariably wave away your apologies with his paw and offer to buy you a beer instead. Harley-Davidsons do strange things to people.

When you have tired of the crush in the streets you can ride on to the beach and join the thousands of others also enjoying their only chance to ride in Florida without a helmet. Though the 10 m.p.h. speed limit is as rigorously enforced as it is everywhere else in the city, by policemen who patrol along the traffic lanes marked in the sand.

Left **Police Chief Paul Crow sums up the new firm but fair attitude towards the visiting motor cyclists in Daytona. 'I'm not so concerned about someone's exhaust system or what kind of handlebars he has, but if a biker thinks it's smart to pop a wheelie on Main Street or run 80 m.p.h. on a public street, he'll find out just how tough we can be.'**

Above **Cruising past Froggy's saloon. Daytona restricts bike parking to the sidewalk and allows cars along Main Street, while Sturgis has a better sense of priority and bans cars and lets the bikes park on the tarmac.**

To get a better view of some of the best two-wheelers in America, a visit to one of the Custom and Vintage bike shows will offer a close-up look at what can be achieved by lavishing years of work or an awful lot of money on a motor cycle. For twenty years the Rats Hole Show has attracted the very best two-wheeled creations and restorations from all over America for one of the most prestigious events in the show calendar that everyone here wants to win. Beside the beach, the long-established boardwalk show hosts a line-up in the hot ocean air, while the Ocean Conference Centre invites people into the cool interior of the building where the Harley-Davidson factory hold a display of their customers' best bikes. All the shows are arranged so that they do not clash on the same day and you will often find the same machine on display at each location. The value and prestige of the prizes are such that even a lowly placing at a show can pay for the vacation.

A few miles past the city limits is the Volusia County Fairground, location of the wall of death, motor-cycle rodeo, vintage bike auctions and home to the 'largest swap meet in the world'. Visitors to Daytona soon become immune to such boasts as many of the events in the state are unashamedly advertised as the largest in the world – but the Swap Meet gets closer to its promoters' claims than most. If you are looking for a hinged rear mudguard for your 1923 JD or the rare oil tank that was only fitted to the 1937 Knucklehead – chances are that you will find it here. There is a rule to be borne in mind though as you sort through dozens of seemingly identical items. 'Let the buyer beware.' Ask three 'experts' if a 1949 Panhead engine will easily fit into a 1938 rigid Flathead frame, and you may get three different answers. (It will if the top tube and seat post tube are notched ¼ inch for clearance – but then I'm just another 'expert'!)

Left **The Rodeo Sweetheart leads the opening parade at the start of the motor-cycle rodeo at the Volusia fairground.**

Some vendors drive down from the northern states with a handful of bikes they have restored over the year, and set up shop outside their vans. While they are eager to make a sale to fund further restorations (particularly 'down south' where they fetch higher prices), making sure that a prospective purchaser would be a suitable new owner is often an important factor in a deal. Anyone with a foreign accent who expresses an interest, though, will often be told that all of the bikes on display have been sold despite 'for sale' signs being posted. No sale is often preferred by the vendors rather than consigning yet another vintage American motor cycle to export from the motherland.

All the shops along the length of Main Street close down for the duration of the motor cyclists' stay and are emptied of their stock, before temporarily letting them out to visiting entrepreneurs who can better cater to the visiting clientele. With the exodus of the local traders – in come the tattooists, T-shirts and chrome accessories and in between the vendors are the bars, crammed to capacity.

One in particular stands out from the modern watering holes and possesses a character that comes from it being a biker bar for all fifty-two weeks of the year. 'The Boot Hill Saloon – across from the cemetery' it says on the T-shirts that seemingly every visitor purchases.

While the old bone yard on the other side of the street may have been the inspiration for the name of the saloon, its overgrown pathways are testament to it having become almost forgotten, while the Boot Hill is now known all over the world. Dennis Maguire who bought the place and renamed it in the early 1970s was a Harley rider, and what was previously just a local bar soon became the visitors' home from home. Situated near the bottom end it soon became the place to meet, as you could park outside at a time when it was prohibited along most of the street.

'Order a drink have a seat – you're better off here than across the street'. You will also be better off here than at many of the other bars for the beer prices are not inflated for Bike Week. Inside the bar most of the furniture is a mass of names and messages that have been crudely carved by the buck knives of past visitors, while the ceiling and walls are decorated with snapshots, T-shirts, underwear and

Above left **The Boothill Saloon. 'It's a bar for motor-cycle enthusiasts and it's going to stay that way. Nothing's going to change,' says the current owner, Art 'Gary' Gehris.**

Left **Typical sign outside a Daytona bar displaying the establishment's house rules. Feuds between rival gangs have been the cause of trouble in the past, but now back patch clubs tend to avoid Daytona because of its restrictions on the wearing of club 'colours'.**

other memorabilia that tell tales of some of the wilder nights that have occurred there and elsewhere.

During the Bike Week, though, there is a large police presence continuously stationed outside all the bars to prevent any partying from getting out of hand, although this invariably has the effect of preventing it from ever really getting started.

Many of the other bars around Daytona that cater to motor cyclists are also just small shacks, but situated in the countryside they have large shady areas behind them in which to hold large events for the influx of visitors. Bands play Southern rock, hogs are roasted, cases of beer are drunk and an awful lot of T-shirts are sold so the folks back home can tell where you have been and why you are walking around for weeks afterwards with a grin on your face.

Competition to attract the dollar is keen and ever more inventive ways of extracting it from visitors are concocted. In fact most of the bars make more money from the sale of drinks and T-shirts during the Bike Week than they do in the rest of the year put together.

The Last Resort on Highway 1 has 'The Hanging Tree' out back. Here during parties a Japanese bike is destroyed by a long queue of people who pay to take it in turns to swing at it with a sledgehammer. When the heap of twisted metal no longer resembles a motor cycle it is then strung up to join the many others suspended in its branches, and a local charity is considerably better off.

The Cabbage Patch Bar puts its own personal touch on the female wrestling competitions that it holds. Instead of the usual mud, jelly or oil used in these slippery bouts, The Cabbage Patch fills the large pit with coleslaw.

The Pub 44 attracted 10,000 people for their big blow-out of the week, which culminated in the destruction of a 750 cc Yamaha. Drained of oil it was started up and jammed on full throttle. Three minutes later the glowing engine exploded in a shower of hot metal, leaving the crowd to finish off the job.

Above left **The Hanging Tree in the Japanese garden behind the Last Resort bar. In the foreground – tonight's sacrifice. The Last Resort is also renowned as the place where the hitchhiking serial killer, 'Aileen Wuornos', spent her last night of freedom, asleep on an old truck seat in the bar.**

Above **You just know that he rides a Harley.**

It's not just Harleys that arrive for the Bike Week – other American motor cycles are welcomed and British ones are accepted. There are a small number of Japanese bikes as well, but they understandably keep a low profile and certainly don't park on Main Street. It is an understatement to say that Japanese motor cycles are disliked by most Harley-Davidson riders in America.

Today the Daytona Bike Week is a well-organized and orderly event, and considering the size it has grown to, is relatively trouble free. Thankfully it has come a long way from the 1970s when it experienced problems that threatened to end it all.

The behaviour of some of the visitors then exceeded the boisterous nature that makes such an event enjoyable and became threatening and troublesome. The response of the police force to this was to come down hard on even the most minor traffic infringements during subsequent years. Tickets were issued like confetti and the police were accused of acting in a manner that was, at best, referred to as heavy-handed. The hassles that all the visitors had to endure became so severe in 1980 that even the motor cycle manufacturers that held shows in the city were discussing a boycott and the possibility of moving the Bike Week to Texas. Not only was it a more central location but it would also be far away from the Daytona police force.

When they heard about the threatened boycott of the event and potential loss of revenue in their city, local businessmen called a meeting with the police chief. C. W. Willits's tight-lipped reply to criticisms of his men's conduct was that 'The city commissioners hired me to enforce the law, they didn't tell me to issue warnings and to turn my back on enforcement.' As a consequence of everyone's concerns about the future of the Bike Week, an uneasy alliance was reached that lasted for several years afterwards.

What could not be ignored though was that the Daytona Bike Week currently brings 200 million dollars flowing into the area's economy over a ten-day period.

When Paul Crow became the police chief in 1989 after having spent six of his twenty-two years in the force as a motor-cycle officer, it was soon apparent that he was willing to work with everyone involved to ensure the resort's biggest money-spinner continued. His approach to the problems that can occur at such an event obviously worked. 'The overwhelming success of my first Bike Week is directly attributable to the respectful courtesy and positive attitudes displayed by participants and the law enforcement officers who interfaced with them.'

The fiftieth anniversary in 1991 was the largest ever and brought 250,000 people to Daytona, while subsequent Bike Weeks hover around the 100,000 to 150,000 level. Despite such large numbers they have been less troublesome than the annual invasion of 'breakers' who replace the motor cyclists when they leave town. With the start of the spring break bringing in tens of thousands of

vacationing college students to the resort at the end of Bike Week – who wants to spend a week in jail with a bunch of kids away from home for the first time!

Above **In common with many American states, Florida has laws for compulsory eye protection, lights on and crash helmets. The helmet law is particularly loathed and there are motor cyclists' organizations fighting to get it repealed. Humans as well as dogs having come to the conclusion that helmet laws suck!**

Right **Nova Campground. 'Yeah, I've enjoyed my Bike Week.'**

LY & RACES

STURGIS

Sturgis nestles in the shadows of the Native Americans sacred Black Hills in South Dakota. The elderly residents who were born here may have come into the world during a peaceful time, but then their parents were certainly around in the days when it was on the very frontier of the old wild west. It was here that 'Crazy Horse' was born, and was a place where the Sioux and Cheyenne could live in relative peace as they still do today. Until, that is, the gold rush of 1872 disrupted their lives for ever. Thousands of miners invaded the area to seek their fortune, closely followed by others whose aim was to relieve those who had struck lucky. It soon became a wilder and more dangerous place, as the army arrived ruthlessly to crush the tribes rising against the invasion of their sacred land, while men fought and killed each other in the mining towns and saloons.

In contrast, when 300,000 motor cyclists invaded the area in 1990 for the fiftieth rally, the only complaint that Mayor Andrew Salivas received was from a woman who could not get to the post office because of all of the traffic. With so many people descending on a small town there are bound to be some incidents that occur, but it is the sense of responsibility of 99 per cent of the rally goers and the tolerance of the residents that continue to make it such a successful and friendly event.

Above **Prior to the evening's racing at the Jackpine Gypsies Short Track circuit, the flags of the state are paraded around the track.**

Left **Dawn – the day before the Bike Week begins, and the first riders arrive on Main Street.**

23

The Black Hills Motor Classic is a year older than the Daytona Bike Week and has become a mecca for Harley-Davidson riders who arrive from all over the world. It has come a long way from the day when a few local riders got together to discuss ways of injecting some more excitement into their lives.

The Jackpine Gypsies Motorcycle Club (initially 'The Rapid City Motorcyclists') were formed on 21 January 1936 when a group of friends in Sturgis elected officers, and their new president arranged their first club event for the following weekend – a coyote hunt aboard motor cycles.

It was the local Indian motor-cycle dealer and president of the club, J.C. 'Pappy' Hoel, who was the inspiration behind the formation of the club and who continued to remain a pivotal figure behind its organization for the rest of his life. He became so well liked and respected during his lifetime, that after his death in 1989 a plaque was attached to the trackside fence at the Jackpine Gypsies Short Track, which proclaims that the empty parking space beside it is permanently reserved for 'Pappy'.

The Gypsies' long-term solution appeared after they discovered

Above **Group shot from one of the earliest Jackpine Gypsies tours to Mount Rushmore. During the early years, all of the visitors to Sturgis could fit into Pappy & Pearl's backyard for the barbecue and camp out.**

Right **'It's a way of life, always has been – always will be.'**

24

Above **A specially modified Sportster comes up to the start to take its chances climbing the steep incline at the Gypsies hill climb.**

a long-forgotten half-mile dirt track at the fairground on the outskirts of town, and set about clearing the scrub away. At first they just raced around it for their own amusement until Pappy persuaded some local businessmen to put up some money to hold an event that would attract racers from all over the state for some real action. 'The Black Hills Motor Classic' was created as a non-profit corporation, and the Jackpine Gypsies' part of the deal was to organize the races while the businessmen recouped their investment by catering to the visitors' needs over a weekend.

When the American Motorcycle Association sanctioned the track for national racing it became a more widely known date in the calendar. As the competitors began arriving from states further afield, so did an increasing amount of motor-cycle clubs and it became renowned as a social event as much as a sporting occasion.

Back then motor-cycle clubs were, for the most part, very formal organizations. Members wore identical uniforms that were almost military in appearance and they invariably rode large Harley-

Davidsons and Indians fitted with windscreens, saddlebags and other touring accessories.

Prizes were awarded for the best turned-out club, smartest club member and best equipped motor cycle, while anyone who left their hat or tie at home felt the shame of having let their friends down. Trophies for the best tattoos and biggest beer gut were many years away and as for a wet T-shirt competition – what was a T-shirt?

The Jackpine Gypsies decided to introduce their visitors to the beautiful scenery around the Black Hills while they were there and held an annual tour around the area on the Friday before the weekend's racing. This culminated in a visit and picnic at Mount Rushmore where the heads of four presidents had been carved into

Left **'Kenny' the scarecrow motor cyclist.**

an outcrop of rock. Before long the weekend in Sturgis was becoming so popular that people began arriving earlier in the week and another tour to the Devil's Tower, a hundred miles away in Wyoming, was added to the itinerary. Both monuments have since become familiar internationally through the films *North by Northwest* and *Close Encounters of the Third Kind*.

Today these tours are still held by the 'Gypsies' as is a full week's programme of races at their half-mile, short track, TT course and hill climb.

The innocence of those early days was not a substitute for having fun, as a visit to the National Motorcycle Museum in Sturgis will prove. Here the pictures and stories from those early years show a large bunch of motor cyclists getting together to enjoy themselves by meeting old friends, making new ones and creating a lot of noise. While such behaviour might be considered inconvenient or disruptive to residents of other small towns the visitors are generally welcomed, or at the very worst tolerated, by the residents. Many of them participate in the running of the Bike Week or welcome the motor cyclists into their homes.

Jean Reede has been accommodating visitors from all over the world for the last fifteen years and her front lawn has become a landmark. 'Kenny', her scarecrow motor cyclist, is brought out of the garage every August and planted on an old motor bike from where he can watch the traffic go by. One year he went missing and the police put out an APB on him, only for him to return the next morning. 'Once the people who took him away had finished with him, they brought him back and threw him into the garden. He was sprawled out on the ground with his limbs askew like an old drunk sleeping off a hangover.'

Some people here return home with a more permanent souvenir that is a constant reminder for the rest of their lives of their visit to Sturgis during Bike Week. Back in the 1960s it is said that some marriages were conducted over a Harley-Davidson technical manual which could be torn up at any time to dissolve the partnership immediately. At Sturgis unions, more legal perhaps in the eyes of God, are conducted outdoors in the park by ministers surrounded by a congregation of V-twins and their leather-clad riders. Fifty to sixty couples every year conduct their nuptials here in front of the minister who reads from a bible that rests upon the seat of the groom's motor cycle.

Left **Minister Mike touts for business. Many couples save their wedding day for August, when they can honeymoon in the Black Hills during Bike Week.**

Many of the visitors to Daytona at the beginning of March travel down from snowbound states in the north and by necessity have to bring their bikes along on trailers, or with a group of friends in converted old school buses. Once there most visitors are content to cruise around the city as all the venues of the Bike Week activities are situated relatively close together.

As Sturgis is more centrally located in the continent and held in August, the summer weather invariably makes riding a couple of thousand miles there as enjoyable as the event itself. After arriving it is tempting to give your engine no time at all to cool off, when faced with so many 'must see' places to visit.

The Black Hills may be sacred to the Native Americans but they are also revered by motor cyclists for the spectacular roads that wind through them and across the surrounding prairies and towns alive with the ghosts of the old west. The tarmac roads may have replaced the old dirt trails but the names of the places they pass still remain – Dead Horse Gulch, One Mule Hill and Horsethief Lake.

The old mining town of Deadwood is the capital of the Black Hills and in its gold-rush days a hundred and twenty years ago it was the scene of the very depths of moral depravity. Today it resembles a wild-west theme park with its main street of wooden-fronted buildings patrolled by policemen on horseback. The gambling saloons that line it have sawdust strewn over the floor, and women wearing period dress and fixed smiles deal the cards and try to relieve you of your vacation money. The 'Last Chance Saloon' is called after miners, who hadn't struck lucky in the hills, made their last attempts to leave town with more than the clothes they stood up in. Next door the Saloon No 10 is the place where Wild Bill Hickok lost more than his shirt and became one of the more infamous gamblers of the day who were carried out feet first. While holding a poker hand of 'Aces and Eights' he was shot in the back of the head by Jack McCall and buried in the local cemetery up on the hill, later to be joined by Calamity Jane. The chair that he had been sitting in at the time is now displayed above the bar and his fatal hand of cards is known to all who chance their luck as 'Dead man's hand'.

Some of the local ladies had another way of relieving visitors of their money in a tradition that was older than the Bike Week itself – but their visible and legal old establishment was shut down by city officials in a puritanical purge a couple of years ago.

Left **Lone rider enjoying the last of the evening's sun. Come night-time and the streets are just as busy until the police decide they want to go to bed and close the show down in the early hours.**

The Rushmore Plaza Civic Centre in nearby Rapid City is renamed Harley-Davidson headquarters for the week and is the focus for all the Harley Owners Group events. In the parking lot outside they hold bike shows and present displays by the Seattle Cossacks and Victor McLagen stunt and drill teams. Inside there are service seminars and opportunities to meet personalities like Peter Fonda and racing star Chris Carr or even the current Ms Harley-Davidson herself. All of the top executives from the company mingle with the crowds and seem genuinely interested in the opinions of their products' owners.

Back on Main Street the procession that began when the sun came up continues unabated until the police close it down at 2 a.m., for they at least have beds to go to.

In between times many of the visitors have a burning desire to be noticed and will go to extraordinary lengths to do so, whether it be by a sidecar outfit with the chair removed and an eighteen-foot canoe bolted on, its two occupants wearing life jackets and working paddles, or a 'buffalo bike' that has a full hide completely covering the vehicle and the head of the luckless previous occupant mounted on the front. Just when you think that nothing else could surprise you, along comes something else that is even more unexpected and unprecedented. If a motor cycle is not built to attract attention, then

Right Just when you think that you have seen it all and nothing else will surprise you, along comes Ron Stratman on his 'Shovelo'. The result of a warm July evening, when a buffalo mated with his 1980 Shovelhead.

Below A Harley-Davidson Servicar that originally had a large box mounted on the back. This has now been removed and a unique pillion seat installed.

Above **'My lizard goes everywhere with me – he's done 9,000 miles, doncha know.'**

Above **Sitting pretty in a side-car, a couple well into the spirit of the event tour the streets. In consideration of the local laws, she has carefully applied small scraps of paper to protect her modesty. No wonder he's smiling.**

Above **The Broken Spoke Saloon and some of its unique décor. Old Harleys, Indians and Excelsiors decorate the walls while drinkers sit around and gaze upwards, wishing it was them who had stumbled across one of these bikes under a tarpaulin in a barn.**

its pillion passenger might make up for it by wearing an outfit that just stops short of breaking the local decency laws. Many people even bring their pets along on their riding vacation, and dogs, snakes and other reptiles are frequent, and seemingly willing, passengers.

The Sturgis Motor Works is owned by Dave Iverson, a collector of vintage American motor cycles and renowned specialist in their restoration. People who arrived in town would invariably drop in to the shop and join others who hung out there, to see what he was currently working on or just to look over his collection of antique

motor cycles. It eventually got to be such a social centre that he capitalized on its popularity by expanding the site and setting up a bar, The Broken Spoke Saloon and Museum, in 1988. The motor-cycle business at the back is thriving: now he can get on with his work, and the bar is the ideal environment for his museum. All around the interior walls are mounted some of his vintage Harley-Davidsons that are waiting for their turn in the workshop, along with ephemera that goes back to the dawn of motor cycling.

There is a variety of food from around the world on sale in the

Above **When the sun goes down, the riders park up for the night and head for one of the bars and an evening's entertainment. At one establishment, 'Boom Boom', the former US ladies wrestling champion takes on all challengers – wrestling in whipped cream.**

Left **There is no other event in the world that could attract such a diverse collection of people and such unique characters.**

street, but it is only the fast variety – pizza, bratwurst, Polish sausage and burritos. The food found on offer at The Road Kill Café, though, is only on the menu presumably because it was not fast enough, and will almost inevitably separate the 'Rich Urban Biker' from the 'One percenter'. Centre line bovine, Outta luck duck and Smidgen of pigeon!

Manageress Peggy Velker sidles up to customers surprised by the fare on offer with phrases like, 'It tastes really neat when it's fresh from the street' and 'It's gotta be tried while it's still in the hide'. Apparently it is all a joke and the dishes are in fact the ordinary café fare of ribs, pancakes and chicken.

'We're just trying to make the best of a bad situation. Nobody likes to run over an animal . . . we want to do for road mishaps what M.A.S.H. did for war!' Vegetarian visitors to Sturgis are advised to bring a week's supply of food with them.

The fiftieth anniversary in 1990 raised many problems when the population of Sturgis was swollen by treble the amount of visitors they were expecting to 300,000. The visiting two-wheelers represented one in thirteen of all motor cycles registered in America.

While it is doubtful that such a large number of people will arrive again for many years, some of the local politicians and businessmen felt it was time to regulate and run the event in a more organized way. So they formed a consortium among themselves to act in the interests of the local community, although their critics claim that they are acting in their own interests while opposing competitors who are not part of their self-appointed organization.

The first change that was made was the fifty-two-year-old name of the Bike Week – from 'The Black Hills Motor Classic' to 'The Sturgis Rally and Races' – and they then went on to create an official logo that they could then license.

The Buffalo Chip campground has long been regarded as the most exciting and best place to stay for visitors. It is almost a town in itself with its own shops, bars, radio station and newspaper. Concerts are held in its large natural amphitheatre and the bands play to an audience seated on motor cycles. Ride in, park in front of the stage, put your feet up on the handlebars and watch the concert and enjoy the music. No matter how good the bands are, though, you will not hear much applause. To elicit an encore the audience start their engines and let their motor cycles roar their approval.

In 1992 the drinks licences for the site were opposed by a few local and influential people. They were joined in their opposition by the manageress of the local film developing company, who offered to show to anyone interested copies of photographs she had depicting motor cyclists participating in behaviour which she did not approve of and did not want allowed.

The 'Chip' claimed to deaf ears that there has never been a single fight at their campground, that it was several miles out of town, and that people who camped there knew what it was like and did so out of choice. A sustained campaign against the 'Chip' was waged that succeeded in making it 'dry' in 1992. Defeated and with attendances considerably down that year, it was reluctantly put up for sale.

President of the new consortium is Gary Lippold who is quite clear in his intent. 'We are going to promote the classic as a more family orientated event.'

A poll conducted amongst the residents and visitors by the local newspaper *The Rapid City Journal* revealed that they did not share

Above **'You ain't havin' fun – til they dial 911,' shouted someone in the crowd. This was a bum rap though. The young lady was getting so much attention as she came down the street on the pillion seat, that the cops figured she must have been showing something that she should not have. As she is being arrested her partner is given directions to the jail house where she can be bailed out. To make a point to the officers, the onlookers promptly had a whip-round for the bail money and the rider rode off clutching a wad of donated bills.**

Left **They may have ridden two thousand miles to get here, but they are not going to stop now, and will cover a few hundred more before it's time to go home.**

the consortium's views and were opposed to their patronizing morality. The overwhelming majority of them wanted the event to stay just as it was – rowdy and a little bit risqué – that they did not want the name of the event changed and that they certainly did not want the event moved to the larger Rapid City, as had been suggested.

Indeed many people are quite indignant that the consortium have set themselves up as moral guardians and overseers of the Bike Week and question their motives for doing so.

The Black Hills Motor Classic will endure. But whether its spirit will be tempered remains to be seen.

RALLIES

THE HARLEY-DAVIDSON ASIA PACIFIC RALLY

Imagine being restricted to living and riding your Harley in one of the smallest and most densely populated cities in the world – and never being allowed out. Such was life for the members of the Hong Kong chapter of the Harley Owners Group (HOG).

There are six million people living in this tiny south-eastern tip of China, in an area that is smaller than New York City and on streets that are even more choked with traffic. Once a month the club would meet for an early Sunday morning ride out before the roads filled up. However, no matter what direction they rode off in, they would always arrive at the sea or the Chinese border in less than forty-five minutes. By 1990 they had grown tired of riding round in circles and looked around for somewhere that would offer a more interesting and lengthy route.

A thorough study of the atlas revealed that the only solution was to ship the bikes to another country and that there was only one destination that had excellent roads and was not politically unstable, too small, too expensive, too far away or under the control of dictators or communists – Malaysia. Faced with the astronomical cost of shipping their bikes to Malaysia they sought sponsorship and found it with Esso of Singapore with additional help from Harley-Davidson and the area's airline and shipping company. In return for making themselves available for some promotional appearances and interviews during the trip, most of their expenses were paid for and the rest of their time was their own.

The bikes were crated up and shipped out to Singapore in advance, where once unpacked they were ridden across the border into Malaysia for their tour. As the country is just north of the equator, it enjoys a tropical climate that encourages the growth of plants which cover two-thirds of the country in a lush and dense foliage. The next ten days were spent riding through the rain forests and rubber plantations and crossing Fraser Hill which has such narrow roads and tight bends that traffic can only travel in one direction at a time. Set times determine which direction that is.

Left **Lunch stop and a rest in the shade on the way to Selengor.**

Below **The Hong Kong HOG riders stop off on the beach for a group shot during the first Asia Pacific Rally.**

The visit to the country's capital, Kuala Lumpur, resulted in the highlight of the trip for the riders. Here they met the Royal Raja Muhda of Selengor, who had heard of the visit of the HOG riders and insisted that they stop by to see him. Malaysia is a country made up of a number of states each with its own royal family. In a country where the principal form of transport is small motor cycles, a Harley-Davidson Heritage Softail is the king of the road. When it is also owned and ridden by royalty, then traffic magically parts, as the sight and sound of the Raja aboard his Harley-Davidson bearing the royal crest cuts an effortless swathe through the crowds.

With the success of their first trip behind them, Hong Kong HOG decided to approach the Chinese authorities for permission to enter their country. After some delicate negotiations they were granted a three-day visa and twenty-two Harleys crossed the border, making history as the first group of foreign motor cyclists to be allowed into the country. The success of this trial visit paved the way for a longer trip to Shanghai for their Second Asia Pacific Rally in 1991. A trip to China and a second tour to another country overseas are now annual dates in their diaries and give them something to look forward to while enduring the choking traffic on those short monthly rides.

THE AUSTRALIAN RALLY SCENE

Whether it's Ponde, Darwin River Rocks, Purga Creek or Aratula, you know what you are going to get for your money at the many events held throughout Australia. Most of them are situated in out-of-the-way places where a lot of noise can be made without upsetting anyone and where no one can wander in by mistake. With several thousand riders turning up and handing their money over at the gate, the entertainment can afford to be lavish. Fireworks, skydivers and drag-racing are common and spectacular sights. While 'The Globe of Death', where two riders circulate inside a fifteen-foot-diameter ball of lattice metalwork, one riding round horizontally and the other vertically, may make an appearance. Usually though, these are just temporary distractions from the serious business of partying and getting wrecked. The strippers are a compulsory attraction and respite from the many bands that play, and they will inevitably ease the crush inside the beer tent when they walk on to the stage. Many clubs turn up for these weekends, and while the atmosphere is wild and loose, they are remarkably friendly and trouble free.

Above **Rider from the Blonks MC of Darwin, Australia.**

Above right **The annual Mildura drag races in Victoria, Australia, and a competitor is pushed on to the start line by his pit crew.**

Below right **Various club members at the Blonks MC clubhouse.**

HOG EUROPEAN RALLY

The Harley Owners Group has become a large and successful organization in America, but over in Europe there has been an eight-year wait for the chance to get started.

The first European rally was held in England in the pouring rain at Cheltenham race course during the summer of 1991. It was an important step into Europe for the company and many of the company's executives made the trip across the Atlantic to be part of it. 'Buying a Harley is an emotional transaction,' says the company president, and to fulfil that transaction they have a committed 'close to the customer' policy. This gives them the opportunity to mingle with the crowds at events like this and listen to the riders whose views and opinions they are keen to hear.

The major HOG rallies like this are distinguished from other rallies of similar size by the facilities that are offered to the visitors.

Here it is not enough just to erect a bar and provide bands as the only entertainment. There are technical seminars, a chance to put questions to the top factory personnel, games, film shows, sporting activities and a crèche for children so that mummy and daddy can enjoy it all unencumbered. Members of the public are encouraged to visit, to look around at the bikes and chat to the owners, which generates a huge amount of good publicity for Harley-Davidsons. Meanwhile the impeccable behaviour of the HOG members and fundraising of large amounts of money for The Muscular Dystrophy Association greatly improve the image of motor cyclists.

The 1992 European rally at Mulhouse on the French side of the border with Germany was also held in the pouring rain. But while it attracted smaller numbers than the 5000 who attended the English rally, there was a greater number of countries represented because of HOG's rapid expansion throughout Europe.

Above **French HOG members. Leather and chains are as much a part of the Harley riders image today as they were forty years ago.**

Left **Like father like son at the HOG European rally in France.**

Right **1952 Panhead and Swedish friends basking in the setting sun.**

THE SWEDISH RALLY SCENE

With such a brief summer between its harsh winters the Swedish Harley rider has to fit a lot of events into a short space of time to get the most out of his riding season. Every weekend there is a major rally somewhere in the country, in addition to the many others in neighbouring countries that try to entice the riders across their border.

The one event that these riders all try to attend is the 'Mälaren Runt' in mid-August, organized by their only Harley-Davidson magazine, *MCM*. Thousands of riders convene in a large car park in Stockholm on the Friday and proceed in a huge convoy to ride the 300 kilometres round the Malaren lake. Riders can stop and camp anywhere they like on the route during the next two days and nights, turning the whole area into a 300-kilometre party. While most other European countries attract around 20 per cent of the Harley-Davidson owners that live within their borders to their largest national events, such is the appeal of the Mälaren Runt that over half of all the Harleys in Sweden turn up for the weekend. Once there they create a laid-back atmosphere that is typical of Scandinavians, and the absence of attitudes gives the event a relaxed feel that is quite unique.

THE EUROPEAN SUPER RALLY

Each year in addition to the many local and national rallies run by the long-established Harley-Davidson clubs in each country, there is a European event which all the member clubs attend.

This began in 1972 at a Dutch rally when the club presidents from Sweden and England called a meeting with the other presidents to put forward their idea about a European rally to be held in a different country every year. Their idea was universally accepted and

Above **Paris Super Rally 1992. As the rallyists were camped around a racetrack, it was only natural that they would race around the circuit during the day. At one point a crowd blocked off a section and stopped everyone who came along, allowing them to continue on their way only after they had performed a burn out.**

Top **The French Harley riders have a sense of style that is quite unique.**

Above **Paris Super Rally. Women now account for 2 per cent of all new Harley-Davidsons sold.**

Right **Winding the power on at the Paris Super Rally.**

the largest annual gathering of European Harley riders was born, the Super Rally.

The first one was held in England the following year, as it was again in 1979, '84 and '89. More recently Belgium, Norway, France and Italy have taken their turn.

The job of organizing the event in 1992 was given to a group of Harley-riding gypsies, the 'Niglo' club. Niglo is the gypsy word for 'hedgehog' which was a source of food that they hunted on their travels in the old days, and is still regarded as a symbol of luck to them. Most of them are entertainers, circus workers or other travelling folk and they are unique for being a club bound by nationality yet have no country. The majority of them though are French, which neatly determined just where the event would be held. They located a racing track on the outskirts of Paris and 8000 people arrived for what turned out to be the largest Harley-Davidson rally ever seen in Europe.

THE GERMAN BIKE WEEK

The German Bike Week organized by 'The Bones MC' is only a recent arrival on the German rally scene. But the three- to-four day meeting has the potential to become the largest event of its kind in the country. It is held on an old dirt track situated on the outskirts of Mannheim and each year it draws in the crowds from further afield as the word spreads and the event expands. What makes it so different from many similar events are the unusual and unexpected features, like the troop of Scottish pipers that circulate around the track to signal the start of the festivities, the club's own hot-air balloons that take to the air twice a day carrying their back patch high over southern Germany, or the trophies that are awarded in the bike shows that are not large pieces of silverware but huge polished animal bones mounted on solid wooden plinths.

Above **Member of the Bones MC, organizers of the German Bike Week.**

Left **Show winners trophies awarded at the German Bike Week.**

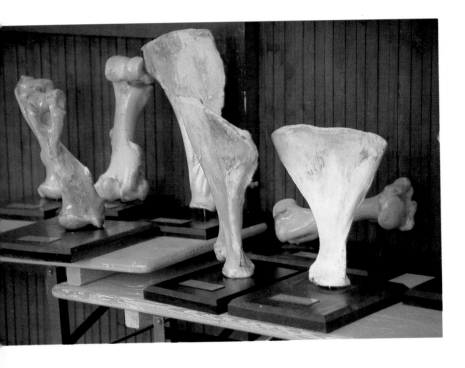

CLASSIC
HARLEY-DAVIDSONS

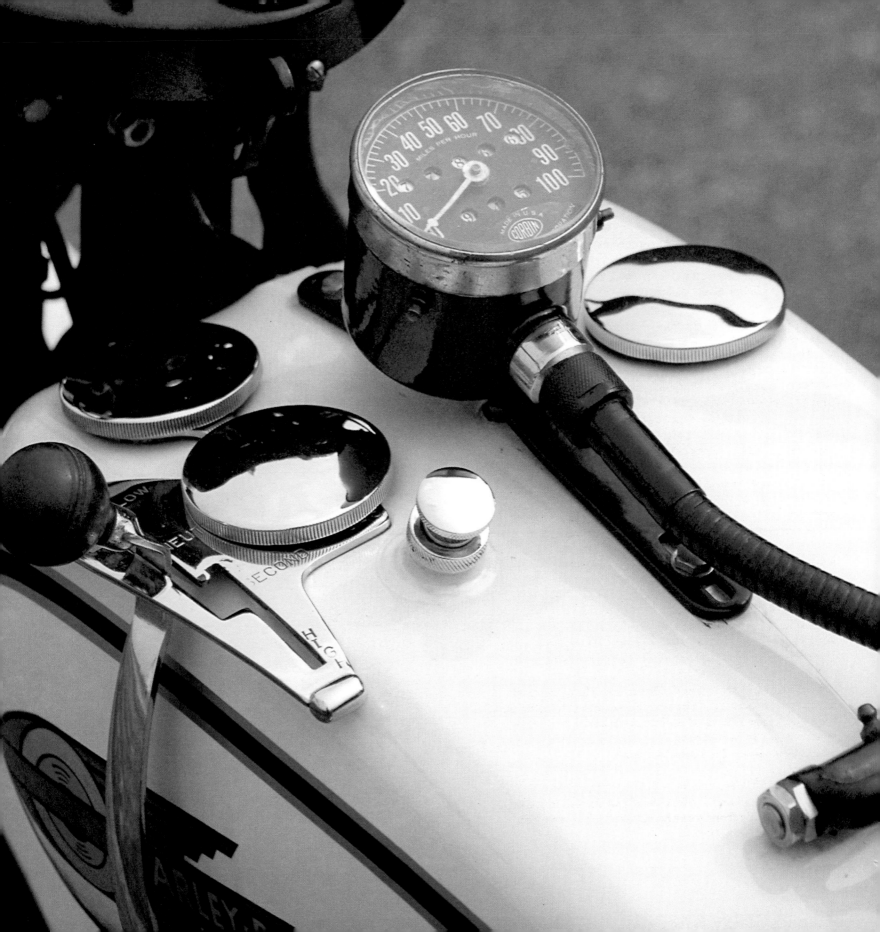

During the early 1900s there were as many as 300 motorcycle companies in America. Most of them were aided in their endeavours by mail-order firms who could supply most of the components required. With a little engineering skill it was possible to produce your own motor cycle from these parts. It may not have been much different from others who had taken the same route, but it did have your name on the tank. Unsurprisingly most of them disappeared just as quickly as they had sprung up and only exist now in photographs. Some lasted for a few years buoyed up by innovations until their innovators turned their attentions to the equally new and exciting world of aviation or the now more dominant motor car. The First World War then saw off most of the others as sales dropped and production was switched to the manufacture of munitions. By the time the depression hit America in 1929 the demise of Excelsior left only two major players, Indian and Harley-Davidson. Through agreement over the introduction of new models and pricing structures, they maintained an uneasy alliance until 1953 when Harley-Davidson stood alone.

Harley-Davidson have in their time produced snowmobiles, golf carts, bicycles, scooters and sold small two-strokes made by Aermacchi in Italy. Indeed for some years in the 1960s their top-selling models were motor cycles of 50 and 60 cc, with the large V-twins only accounting for a third of their annual sales. In the 1920s and 30s they also made 21 cu. in (350 cc), 30.50 (500 cc) singles and very briefly a 35.6 cu. in (584 cc) flat twin. These were primarily for export and, in the case of the smaller single, only achieved significant domestic success in racing and hill-climb competitions.

The 45-degree V-twin and the Harley-Davidson are synonymous with each other. The look, sound and charisma of this engine is the basis for their unique and timeless appeal.

It is an American tradition to measure the capacity of an engine by the cubic inch and not the cubic centimetre. Therefore for 45 cu. in read 750 cc; 55 cu. in, 883 cc; 61 cu. in, 1000 cc; 74 cu. in, 1200 cc; 80 cu. in, 1340 cc.

Following the history of each model are the letter designations which distinguish each model in the range, followed by dates of important, and predominantly exterior, changes and refinements.

Left **Detail of a 1936 model V. This was the last year that any of their motor cycles had a speedometer mounted on the tank. From 1937 all of their models had the speedometer set into a console on the tank, as introduced on the Knucklehead the previous year.**

Right **1992 FLST Heritage Softail. One of several 'retro' looking models in Harley-Davidson's current model range. The Hydra-Glide front forks have been a consistent feature in their line up since 1949.**

PRELUDE

The internal combustion engine that arrived at the dawn of the twentieth century sent many young entrepreneurs scurrying to their garden sheds to pore over its blueprints and concoct their own uses for it. Motor cars and marine engines were the results of some of the earliest efforts.

But for ease of transport along the old wagon trails that existed then, a motor-powered bicycle was regarded as the natural successor to the horse. To this end, Bill Harley and the three Davidson brothers Arthur, Walter and William pooled their talents and resources to form the Harley-Davidson Motor Company.

THE FIRST HARLEY-DAVIDSONS, 1903 to 1918

Their first rolling prototype utilized the De Dion-type engine that was also the basis for most of the other motor cycles that emerged in those pioneering days, and allegedly had an empty tomato can as a carburettor! This single-cylinder machine that made its début in 1903 was only 10.2 cu. in (167 cc) and it powered a leather belt that ran from the engine around a hub on the rear wheel. With some furious pedalling the single-speed engine would fire into life, and at speeds of up to 25 m.p.h., the rider was transported into the modern age.

Soon afterwards they produced a second prototype, made this time with a much larger pocket valve (or IOE – inlet over exhaust) engine, 24.74 cu. in (405.41 cc). Satisfied with its performance, they used it as the basis for their first two production motor cycles that followed later in the year. Sales rapidly multiplied each year and for a long time, just like today, there was a buyer waiting for each one. With the inclusion of the V-twin from 1911 production was: 1905, 8 motor cycles; 1908, 450; 1911, 5,625; 1914, 16,284.

During these early years manufacturers expended large amounts of time, money and effort on racing to enhance their name, and if that failed to capture the public's attention, then the paintwork of their models, bright red (Indian) or yellow (The Flying Merkel) or sporty exhaust-

Right A 1912 Silent Grey Fellow that is about to participate in the 'Pioneer Run' for pre World War One motor cycles. This takes place in England every spring and attracts over 300 machines to ride the 50 miles from London to the South Coast.

sound hopefully would. Harley-Davidson rode a different road. They refused to back racers – even though private entrants frequently won riding their machines. They painted their motor cycles grey and they claimed they were the quietest and most reliable models available.

Hardly the sort of stuff to fire the blood, but for the gentleman seeking a dependable form of transport it was among the best on the market. It was also these qualities that brought it to the attention of those who could place large orders, like police forces, the military and the US post office who ordered 4,800 in one go for their rural postal carriers. All those customers continued their patronage over many years with large repeat orders.

'The Silent Grey Fellow', as these early singles became known, were renowned for their quiet exhaust note, colour scheme and

reliability. This was no idle boast, for the first of the two production models built in 1903 was still running in 1913 after having passed through several owners' hands and covering 100,000 miles. Their first

Below 1912 Silent Grey Fellow. New features and improvements were frequently added during the early years. Semi-valanced front fender, lower lever that operated a rear hub clutch, a seat post mounted on a long spring and a redesigned top rail that allowed the tank to slope downwards at the rear and gave a lowered seating position – all appeared for the first time this year on their Singles and V-twins.

models were actually black and the 'Renault grey' colour was not introduced until 1906, but the nickname was applied to all of their singles that followed.

In what was to become typical of Harley-Davidson's approach, while others expanded their range by offering machines of different sizes, they stuck with the one model and slowly and carefully refined and enlarged the engine over several years. Ninety years later Harley-Davidson still continue a policy of gradual growth. Their current range of twenty-two motor cycles has only two different engines among them.

Prior to 1908, Harley-Davidson had no model designations. From 1908 to 1915 they were based on a system that subtracted 4 from the number of the year. For example, take a Model 6A: 6 means that it was made in 1910 and A refers to the motor cycle. These early singles were generally designated A, B or C models.

1909 30.16 cu. in model introduced
1913 5-35 model introduced; 5 hp from a 35 cu. in engine
1916 to save costs, the single was fitted into the V-twin frame

FIRST V-TWINS, 1909 to 1930

It was inevitable that no sooner had the first motor cycles taken to the road, than engineers were looking at ways to make more powerful engines. The simplest way to do this was to fill the empty space in the frame with a second cylinder. It was also the most practical solution. Taking a single-cylinder engine and attaching another cylinder meant that the horsepower could be doubled at the expense of little extra weight. Soon most of the motor-cycle companies came up with their own version. Harley-Davidson were not about to be left behind and taking their single as a starting point they grafted on an identical cylinder.

After offering this, their first 45-degree V-twin for sale to the public in 1909, they then had promptly to withdraw it for a rethink. While their early single-cylinder motor cycles had performed admirably with a belt drive, the increase in power made by the larger V-twin engine meant that the leather belt was less than effective. Negotiating a steep incline or carrying a heavy load would considerably reduce the rider's progress or even worse, bring him to a stop while the engine ran on uselessly.

Two years later it re-emerged from the workshops, this time with a belt tensioning device to take up any slack and enabling it to cope with the 7 hp engine and speeds up to 65 m.p.h. In a rush of innovation leading up to the First World War it was the recipient of many improvements. The chain drive soon replaced the belt, a clutch and two- then three-speed transmission was fitted, and the frame –

Right 1914 61 cu. in V-twin. Harley-Davidson were now responsible for a third of all new motor cycles that were sold in the US. With riders being enticed into one of their 800 dealerships by advertisements claiming that the Harley-Davidson 'is nature's envoy to you' and that it would carry the rider 'into a land of perpetual welcome'.

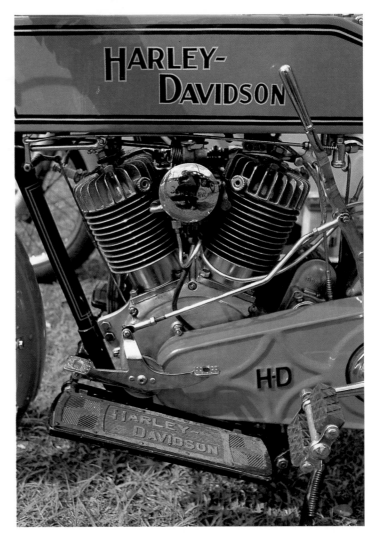

instead of an updated bicycle one – was redesigned the better to cope with the demands made by a large engine. As an option with side-car outfits in mind, it was available with a larger engine bore – either 49.48 cu. in (810.83 cc) or 60.32 (988.55 cc).

Determining the power of these early motor cycles is difficult. America had a method of dividing motor cycles into power groups for the purposes of taxation and insurance. To keep these extra expenses to a minimum, the claimed horsepower of motor cycles was often less than half of the genuine output while the top speeds claimed, by Harley-Davidson anyway, were generally accurate.

Harley-Davidson had contributed 20,000 motor cycles to the allied forces during the war in the military livery of 'olive drab' paintwork. At the time when Henry Ford's words, 'any colour you

Below **1914 V-twin. The spiralling sales of their Singles and V-twins resulted in over 16,000 motor cycles being sold this year. Now that they had such a strong production base in America, the decision was made to follow Indian, Excelsior and Pope into the export market and Harley-Davidson's first dealerships were set up in Europe. A total of 350 motor cycles were shipped across the Atlantic before the outbreak of war curtailed any further exports. This is one of those early imports which arrived in England in 1914, although it has been perhaps 'over restored' more recently. It would be a terrible shame if it was destined to become just a museum piece and never fired up.**

want . . . as long as it's black', informed his customers of their options, a similar phrase echoed in the Harley-Davidson dealerships where the high-gloss olive finish was the only colour officially offered from 1917 to 1932. There was only a brief respite from 1922 to 1924 when a variation, 'Brewster green', temporarily replaced it.

The pre-war boom in motor cycle sales was followed by a dramatic fall afterwards. A brief depression and affordable cars sent most of Harley-Davidson's competitors to the wall and over a half of the company's employees left the factory gates for the last time.

D: 49.48 cu. in model
E–J: 60.34 cu. in model

1912   suspension first provided by a coiled spring inserted into the seat post. First clutch fitted
1914   first footboards, brake and clutch pedals fitted
1915   three-speed transmission available and the inlet rocker arms and pushrods were exposed on the outside of the engine

THE FD & JD MODELS, 1921 to 1929

The basic design of the 61 cu. in pocket valve engine had long since proved to be of sound construction and for the remainder of its run only minor changes were enough to sustain the model throughout the 1920s.

The 61 cu. in F and J (all models in this range referred to as F heads) still remained in the line-up, with the J having a generator instead of a magneto ignition. But an increase in the bore and stroke

of the engine augmented the range with 74 cu. in versions, the FD and JD. Output was now officially claimed to be 18 hp but this was obviously still an underestimate for they could achieve 70 m.p.h.

While the size of the motor-cycle market in America was declining, Harley-Davidson kept their sales figures steady by establishing export markets throughout Europe, Scandinavia, Japan and New Zealand and made forays into Africa.

Twin Cams had been a feature in their racing bikes for ten years before they were installed in a road-going model in 1928. When they were fitted to the JH and JDH they achieved an almost legendary reputation. While they were far superior in performance to almost anything else on the road, their status was enhanced by their scarcity and high cost (20 per cent higher than standard models).

F & J: 61 cu. in models with a magneto ignition or generator
FD & JD: 74 cu. in models in the same alternatives as above
JL & JDL: special sport solo models that were tuned versions of the J & JD
JH & JDH: two cam versions of the 61 – J and 74 – JD engines

1920 the headlight and horn swapped places, the headlight was now mounted above the horn
1921 fully valanced front mudguards fitted
1925 new frame, shaped saddle, elongated teardrop-shaped tank and fatter tyres fitted
1928 front brake standard. 'Two cammers' fitted with a slimmer tank and 18-inch wheels, 2 inches smaller than other F & Js
1929 four-tube silencer appeared on all models and only lasted one year

Left **1928 JDH 'Two Cammer'. The fastest production motor cycle in the world during the two years that it was available. Treated right it could touch 100 m.p.h. although its reliability at high cruising speeds was not to be counted on. This was the end of the road for the 'F head' V-twin as it was superseded by the Side Valve engines.**

Right **1929 model D. Here can be seen the vertical generator that inspired the jibes of the 'three cylinder Harley' and the twin headlights that was a feature on all Harley-Davidsons for two years.**

THE 45, 1929 to 1951

While the overhead valve engines that the British manufacturers produced were obviously the future for motor cycling, they had not reached the stage of mechanical refinement that the side valves had. As they contained many more internal parts their reliability was questioned, while the exposed valve gear was noisy and allowed oil mist to cover the engine and rider. Harley-Davidson stuck to what they knew best and replaced the old IOE F head V-twins with another 45-degree V-twin, the side-valve 45 cu. in D model.

They were no match for Indian's 101 Scout, being 20 m.p.h. slower but their eventual reliability and longevity became legendary and the engine continued in production for forty-three years, latterly in the Servicar.

The generator was vertically mounted on the front left side of the crankcase so that the engine would fit into the existing frame that the 21 cu. in singles were housed in. But to detracting Indian riders, it looked, from a brief glance, like a third cylinder.

It was and still is typical of the company to introduce new models that utilize features from its predecessor or other models in the range. Once established they can be improved and refined in a gentle progression over subsequent years.

Such an evolutionary approach to the introduction of new models and features on their motor cycles continues to this day.

The D engine was rechristened the R when in 1932 it gained a new frame that was bowed at the front and gave space for the generator to be mounted horizontally on the front of the engine in a more conventional position.

When it too had the recirculating oil system installed in 1936, it was given a W prefix. During the late 1930s an overhead valve prototype of the W was produced and underwent tests. The cost, however, proved too prohibitive and it was cancelled in 1940.

It became difficult to distinguish between some of the 45s and the larger 74 and 80 cu. in side valves, for on the outside they were almost identical in appearance. The most obvious difference was that the rear chain on the 45 was on the right while the 74 and 80 had theirs on the left.

From 1932 until 1973 the Servicar, a trike powered by the WS engine and equipped with a large box on the back, was sold to auto shops, small businesses and police forces. With only minor updates it remained virtually unchanged throughout its life. In countries such as India they are still at work, having been converted into taxis that can carry up to eight people.

D: standard model
DS: same as the D but geared for side-car use
DL: same as the D but with high-compression cylinder heads
DLD: same as the DL but with even higher compression heads, larger carburettor and a change in the gearing for enhanced performance
R, RS, RL, RLD: specification as for the above D models
W, WS, WL, WLD: specifications as for the above D models
WR, WLDR, RLDR: 'R' for racing versions of the above

1929   twin headlights were fitted across the range of side valves for this and the following year
1931   received a single-tube silencer instead of twin tubes
1933   all frames and forks across the range are painted black from now on and convex lenses are put on all the headlights
1937   horizontal cooling fins are added to the sides of the cases

Left 1941 WLDR. This was listed as a road model, but internally it was not dissimilar to the competitive Class C racing bikes – the WR and WRTT. During the late 1930s an Overhead Valve prototype of the '45' successfully completed some extensive road tests, but the cost of manufacturing it was too high and the project was dropped. Teardrop-shaped chrome name-plates were a new feature on all models in 1940 and the following year these were supplemented with a chrome strip that ran around the tank.

THE V and U Models, 1930 to 1948

Harley-Davidson hailed the model V, at its launch in 1929, as the greatest achievement in motor-cycling history. While the 74 cu. in engine, frame and front forks were all new, it was a similar side-valve design to the existing '45' and retained its total loss oil system.

This 'greatest achievement' was soon withdrawn from sale with innumerable mechanical problems. The following year it appeared again, but this time heralded by a more muted fanfare.

Many prospective customers were disgruntled that they had not been able to get one of the short-lived 'two cammers' which had been discontinued after just two years and that they were now offered a VL that was 120 lb heavier, not much faster and seemingly unreliable. Within time it was acknowledged that the mechanical durability of the revered 'two cammers' was inferior to the V model, and as the performance of the V model was steadily improved, it was accepted as a worthy replacement. The model was further enhanced by its enlargement to 80 cu. in in 1936 and an optional fourth gear was added, and the following year it gained the recirculating oil and dry sump system that first appeared on the Knucklehead. These carried a new designation – the Model U.

Harley-Davidson sales in 1933 had plummeted to 3,703 from a high of 23,354 in 1926 and there was speculation that the company might be wound up. They managed to remain afloat during the rest of the decade, until the Second World War enabled them to work to capacity again. In the meantime they earned further revenue from the sale of blueprints to a Japanese company. As foreign motor cycles

Above **1936 Model V. This was the last year for the model V engine and the single loop frame that it was contained in. For 17 years Harley-Davidson had produced motor cycles solely in 'Olive Drab' paint, but in 1932 a variety of colours and Art Deco tank designs were applied to all of their models. This particular tank design first appeared in 1936.**

Right **1947 74 cu. in UL. The model U was the last of the large capacity side valve engines that Harley-Davidson made and became a great favourite for the rider who wanted a strong workhorse. While the V had earned a good reputation after its early problems had been sorted out. This was soon eclipsed by the superlatives applied to the model U which had inherited some of the best features of the Knucklehead, the frame, oil system, instruments and tubular front forks, and retained the proven rugged reliability and ease of maintenance of the side valve engine.**

could no longer be imported into Japan, they built their own from Harley-Davidsons plans. From 1935 to 1959 they were completely made from Japanese parts and the finished motor cycles were sold under the name Rikuo (meaning 'King of the road').

V, VL: standard model and high-compression version
VM, VLM: magneto-equipped version of the above
VS: side-car model
VC, VCR: lower than standard compression models for commercial use
VLH, VHS: 80 cu. in sports and side-car geared models
U, UL, US, ULH, ULS etc.: as above but with the new oil system

1931 single headlamp re-fitted and round tool box replaced by a wedge-shaped one across the range of models

1933 colour options instead of the 'Olive Drab' standard were officially offered across the range
1936 a four-speed gearbox was available as an option
1937 the 45, 74 and 80 side valves all came with the Knucklehead's petrol tank with the instruments set in, as well as its double loop frame

Below **This is one of the early versions of the XA Model, fitted with the 15-inch disc wheels and featured a throttle on the left and the hand clutch on the right. Later models reverted to wire wheels and came with an extra shock absorber mounted on the springer forks.**

MILITARY MODELS

During the Second World War Harley-Davidson manufactured almost 90,000 motor cycles for the allied forces. Many of these were never taken out of their crates and in the postwar years were converted to civilian trim and sold to the public. That for each motor cycle made enough spares were produced to build twenty more, means that even today it is almost feasible to build a new WLA from existing 'new' parts. Apart from the WLA, there were also small numbers of their side-valve models and OHV Knuckleheads utilized by the allies.

Much rarer among military motor cycles is the 45 cu. in XA model. The US government had asked Harley-Davidson and Indian to build some shaft-driven motor cycles, and offered them several options. Harley-Davidson chose to make a copy of the German BMW R75–5 while Indian went for a transverse V-twin, the 841. Once they had each built 1,000 motor cycles the Army would then evaluate their performance and make its choice. The contract would then be awarded to whichever was deemed to be the most suitable. When the order was completed the Army decided that it only wanted the WLA 45.

The XA had a lot going for it. As the engine was a horizontally opposed twin it enjoyed better air cooling and, new for Harley-Davidson, had a hand clutch and foot gear change. A shaft drive required less maintenance and was more practical than a rear chain, as on the WLA, particularly in sandy environments where a chain had only a limited working life.

The XA used more precious aluminium and cost significantly more than the WLA and it would take a further year to enter mass production. The WLA was already fulfilling the forces' needs and the end of the desert war made a shaft drive less of a pressing requirement. Faced with these facts, the Army dropped the project.

WLA: American Army's equipped version of the WL
WLC: Canadian Army's version of the WLA
WSR: WS side-car outfit supplied to the Russian forces
ELC: military EL Knucklehead model
UA: military U model

1942 all WLAs from 1942 onwards carried the designation 42 WLA

Right **WLA and owner at the Rats Hole Show in Daytona. The metal rod that sticks up from the handlebars was designed to prevent the decapitation of the rider – by breaking any wire that enemy troops might tie across the road.**

KNUCKLEHEAD, 1936 to 1947

The 61 cu. in Knucklehead that rolled out of the factory in 1936 was the first large overhead valve engine that Harley-Davidson had ever made for the domestic market. Ten years earlier they had begun to make OHVs but only as 21 cu. in singles that were primarily aimed at the Australian and European markets. These had never really sold well at home where a 45 cu. in was considered the minimum practical engine size.

Typically it was available in two versions: the standard model 'E'

and the 'EL' with high-compression pistons. This sportier version would produce 40 hp at 4800 r.p.m. and could manage 95 m.p.h. on a good day. In comparison the established 74 cu. in Model V side valve had only 30 hp at its disposal and its top speed was 10 m.p.h. lower. Its nickname was applied by customers who noticed the similarity of its rocker covers to the knuckles of a clenched fist.

Many of the features it had soon found a place on the side-valve models as they too got the new tank and instrument panel, and large oil tank underneath the seat. While the Knucklehead had recirculating

Left **1941 FL Knucklehead engine. The rocker boxes that resemble the knuckles of a clenched fist can be clearly seen here. The ribbed timing case covers first appeared on the 1940 models, and were redesigned the following year to cope with the extra stress created by the engine being enlarged to 74 cu. in.**

Below **1941 EL Knucklehead. This model produced nearly double the horsepower of the 61 cu. in side valve. Consequently many side valve aficionados, who were perfectly content just to roll along gently, regarded the loud and brash Knucklehead as a 'hooligans' motor cycle.**

oil instead of the total loss system used on the pre-1937 side valves, early models consumed oil, leaks were common and it was renowned for leaving drops on the ground wherever it stood for brief periods. It was, though, a very sound and reliable mount and enhanced its reputation in 1937 when a tuned model set a new speed record of 136 m.p.h.

In time the Knucklehead received the customary increase in engine capacity and the 74 cu. in models joined the line-up in 1941. These were good for an honest 100 m.p.h. and filled the gap when the 80 cu. in Model U was dropped from the line four years later. The 74 was barely able to enter full production when the USA was dragged into the war and the factory almost totally switched to making WLAs for the Army. When peace was again declared, the 74

had just a two-year run until it was discontinued to make way for the Panhead.

E: standard 61 cu. in model
EL: high compression Sports model
ES: fitted with gearing for side-car use
F, FL, FS: 74 cu. in models

1938 valves received full enclosure
1940 fins appeared on the crankcase covers and chromed name plates were fitted on all models, D-shaped floorboards replaced the rectangular ones on all models
1941 the first year that the metal band that ran around the petrol tank appeared on all models in the H-D range

THE PANHEAD, 1948 to 1965

Tここ is a saying that the sometimes temperamental Knuckleheads 'were gnarly, while the Panheads were perfection'.

Harley-Davidson had an excellent engine design right from the beginning of its run and most of the improvements made during its lifetime were consequently directed to other areas.

This was a lighter engine than the all-iron Knucklehead, mainly owing to the use of aluminium for many of its components. On top, the new rocker covers helped the engine to run cooler and their appearance of looking like upside-down baking pans gave the model its unofficial name.

The new hydraulic valve lifters that were fitted inside eliminated the sound of the tappets as well as the need for adjustment – it was also considerably quieter. The traditional springer forks that had been a feature of their machines for so many years lasted for only one year on the Panheads – until hydraulic front forks were fitted on the 1949 model and it was christened the 'Hydra-Glide'. Further new names for Panhead models were to follow. Harley-Davidson had always had a tradition of making rigid-framed motor cycles, and apart from the front forks the only other form of comfort for the rider travelling over rough roads were springs inside the seat post which had first featured on their 1912 V-twin.

This tradition had changed first on the Model K in 1952, and then on the big twin in 1958 when the Panhead was also given a swing arm and shock absorbers, the 'Duo-Glide'.

For the last year of its seventeen-year run it gained an electric starter and was rechristened the Electra-Glide. Statistically it is still with us. The Evolution-engined Softail Heritage was styled to look like the early Hydra-Glide and it was this model that was primarily

Left **1948 EL 'Panhead'. First year of the 'Panhead' and last for the Springer front forks. These 'leading link' front forks had been a constant feature on Harley-Davidsons for forty years. The new telescopic forks on the Hydra-Glide the following year were a tremendous improvement, yet there was no immediate need to introduce suspension to the frame as well, as the sprung seat could smooth out the most rutted roads.**

Right **Here can be seen the other versions of the 'Panhead'. In the foreground a 1965 Electra-Glide with the battery under the seat. Behind a blue 1963 Duo-Glide with rear suspension and behind that a red 1957 Hydra-Glide with a rigid frame.**

responsible for the turnaround in the company's sales in the late 1980s.

E: 61 cu. in
EL: high compression sports model
ELS: fitted with gearing for side-car use
F, FL, FLS: 74 cu. in models
FLH: with a new bottom end in 1955 this became the top of the range version of the 74

1952   first year for the optional foot shift/hand clutch and the last for the 61 cu. in versions
1953   introduction of the distinctive trumpet-shaped horn
1963   oil lines that were previously internal were moved outside the engine

Below **1955 55 cu. in KH model on display at the National Motorcycle Museum in Sturgis. The 1950s was a bad period for the company. They had dropped the 45 cu. in W model and the K model was unable to keep the company buoyant in the middleweight market. Cheaper and faster British motor cycles were flooding the American market and annual sales plunged to 10,000.**

Right **In the pits at a vintage racing event. A closer look at the crankcase of this model K dirt tracker will reveal a crack wide enough to put your fingers in. Proof that while these old motor cycles are cherished by their owners, once on the track they are still ridden to, and beyond, their limits.**

MODEL K, 1952 to 1956

The 750 cc W model may have helped to win the war for America but it was losing the battle for sales in the marketplace to the British motor cycles in the postwar years.

To combat these imports Harley-Davidson replied with the 750 cc model K in 1952. It introduced several new features not seen before on one of their machines, yet many of them common on the foreign interlopers. Notably the four-speed gearbox was worked with a hand clutch and right-foot gear shift, while the handling was improved by the installation of a swing arm and coiled-spring rear suspension. Progressive though these improvements were, the new unit construction engine was still an old-fashioned side valve, and performance was not that much better than the W model it was replacing and still sluggish in comparison to the imports.

The K was soon joined by a more powerful sibling, the KK, which contained the polished ports and cam from the KR racing version but only a small number ever reached the showroom.

1954 heralded the arrival of the 883 cc KH. This had been enlarged by increasing the stroke of the engine, which enabled it to keep up – just about – with its rivals. The following year it was finally

capable of overtaking many of them when an additional model was launched, which also contained the racing parts that were fitted to its sporting predecessor.

The side-valve days were over and the K model out of date before it was even launched. Harley-Davidson had intended it to be just a temporary model until they had perfected a new overhead valve engine to rival the foreign competition. It was barely able to fulfil its function in this respect and the company suffered a great drop in sales as prospective buyers turned their attentions to imported models.

The road-going model struggled to keep up on the road during its five-year production run. The racing version had to remain competitive for the next seventeen years until it could be replaced by the XR 750.

K: standard 45 cu. in model
KK: sportier version of the K
KH: standard 55 cu. in model
KHK: sportier version of the KH
KR: dirt-racing version that came with the option of a bolt-on, rigid rear frame and had no brakes
KRTT: TT and road racing bike with brakes, swing arm and rear suspension
KRM: rare KRTT model equipped for desert racing

Below **In the foreground is an XLH carrying all of the touring extras, while behind it a later XLCH shows the Sportster in its leaner and more potent guise.**

THE SPORTSTER, 1957 to 1985

Harley-Davidson's practice of evolving new models out of old resulted in the début of the XL Sportster in 1957. The factory had invested a lot of money in the machinery and design of the short-lived KH model which they could not afford to write off. Instead they utilized what they had and converted the side-valve design into an overhead valve engine. The 55 cu. in XL Sportster may have been a modified KH but it soon bore absolutely no relation to its predecessor.

The introduction of the XLCH the following year left the competition far behind and was truly the world's first superbike.

When *Cycle World* magazine tested the 1962 model they claimed it to be the fastest production motor cycle that they had ever ridden, capable of 122 m.p.h. and 14-second quarter-mile times. 'It will make hair grow on your chest,' said the writer in awe, 'and

Below **XR-1000. Its twin Dell'Orto carburettors stick out on the right of the engine while the twin exhausts run high along the left of the bike. If it was tuned with instructions from the factory and had enough money thrown at it, it could produce over 100 b.h.p.**

if you already have hair – it will part it down the middle.'

It had been conceived as an off-road competition model and was equipped to handle rough terrain with its knobbly tyres, small peanut tank, magneto, high-level exhaust pipes and no lights. So many riders were soon adding a battery, lights and a silencer that the factory promptly saved them the trouble and brought out a street-legal version in 1959.

In 1972 the engine was given a bigger bore that enlarged it to 61 cu. in but by then the brute had been tamed by noise and emission laws and despite the extra cubes it was slower than the original version of fifteen years before. In 1979 the XLCH was erased from the production schedule, a shadow of its former self, while the other more sedate and refined Sportsters models lasted until they were superseded by the Evolution models.

There were two short-lived versions of the Sportster that were attempts to live up to the racy name. The XLCR-Café Racer featured a frame that retained the front part from the XL which was then mated to a triangular rear section from the racing XR–750 bike, from which it also inherited the rear fender and seat unit. It looked mean and fast in an all-black livery and quite unlike any other Harley before or since – but underneath it was just a standard XL engine that was dressed up for the occasion.

The XR–750 was also the basis for the XR–1000. Taking a basic XLX model as a starting point and bolting on the racer's cylinders, heads and twin carburettors and high-level exhausts resulted in a very fast, but also very expensive, motor cycle. The Café Racer was withdrawn just two years after it first appeared in 1977 but not before the frame had been passed on to the rest of the Sportster range in 1978, while the XR–1000 lasted for an equally brief run that was terminated in 1985.

XL: standard Sportster
XLT: touring model with 3.5-gallon petrol tank
XLX: budget Sportster that replaced the XL
XLH: XL with higher compression launched in 1958
XLS: a 'Customized' XL, with flat bars, sissy bar, highway pegs and slightly extended front forks
Roadster version had buckhorn bars and large tank

1962 was the first year of the short dual exhaust pipes
1967 electric start was introduced
1972 all models enlarged to 61 cu. in
1975 gearshift moved to the left
1978 dual front disc brakes and siamesed exhausts on all models. All XL models received the Café Racer frame
1984 reverted back to one front disc!

Right **Early 'Generator' Shovelhead engine (with the flat timing case) that was carried over from the Panhead that lasted from 1966–69, when it was updated to an alternator.**

THE SHOVELHEAD, 1966 to 1983

The 74 cu. in FL engine continued a pattern of progress that began with the Knucklehead in 1936. In 1966 it was given a top end that had rocker boxes instead of covers, and the shape of them – like the backs of shovels, again provided the source for a new tag.

These early 74 cu. in Shovelheads had the same bottom end as the Panhead and retained the generator mounted on the front of the engine.

This changed in 1970 when it was replaced with an alternator, and points were installed inside the cases to produce a distinctive cone shape to the side of the timing case. Early and late models became known as either 'Generator Shovels' or 'Cone Shovels'.

These early models continued the touring tradition and became

Below **1971 FX Super-Glide. The 'boat tail' fibreglass seat unit that appeared on this model when it was launched was also an option on the Sportster that year, but was universally unpopular and was dropped the following season for a more conventional seat unit.**

larger and more heavily equipped, to the point where they exceeded 750 lb in weight.

FL: standard 74 cu. in version
FLH: high compression 74 and 80 cu. in model
FLT: 80 cu. in engine in new rubber-mounted frame with a modern fairing
FLHT: FLT with traditional handlebar fairing

1969   the first large coloured fairing appeared on the FLH
1972   hand shift was no longer an option as all models converted to foot shift
1978   80 cu. in engine first offered in the FLH
1980   first five-speed gearbox in the range on the FLT
1983   belt drive fitted to the FLH

Above **FXB Shovelhead and FXDB Evolution. The FXB that reintroduced the belt drive to a Harley-Davidson was introduced in 1980 and nicknamed the Sturgis. The Evolution Sturgis behind it was a limited edition in 1990 to commemorate the 50th anniversary of the Bike Week in South Dakota.**

For years the prospective Harley-Davidson owner had a choice of either a huge ponderous bike like the Electra-Glide laden with touring equipment or the slim and lightweight (for Harley-Davidson) Sportster.

During the sixties the chopper cult had become more than a

brief West Coast fashion and, fuelled by the release of the *Easy Rider* film, it soon became a worldwide phenomenon.

While this was happening, Harley-Davidson deliberately remained apart and made no attempts to capitalize on the interest shown in these bikes. Indeed many dealerships refused to work on them or welcome their owners into their shops. People who wanted a customized bike would invariably purchase a second-hand Harley-Davidson, buy custom parts from one of the independent suppliers that had sprung up and patronize one of the bike shops that had taken advantage of the situation and opened their doors solely to cater to this market.

It eventually reached the point when Harley-Davidson could ignore it no longer and the newly appointed designer Willie G. Davidson, grandson of one of the founders, kick-started Harley-Davidson into the modern age.

The result was the FX Super-Glide in 1971, and it was a perfect blend of what the company had to offer. It took the Electra-Glide as a starting point and stripped away the electric start, fairing and touring accessories. Also left off were the fat front forks and in their place were fitted the slimmer versions from the Sportster. At 540 lb in weight it emerged from the workshop having shed more than 200 lb.

So successful was this first step into the custom market that other variations followed. In 1978 another major step forward was made when the FXS Low Rider arrived. This was an FX that had been lowered 2.3 inches, fitted with flat bars and had its forks raked even further forward and shortened, increasing the wheelbase.

FX: 74 cu. in Super Glide
FXE: E for electric starter. Fitted with a slimmer tank and the instruments mounted on the bars
FXEF: 'Fat Bob'. FXE with large dual petrol tanks that had the instruments set onto them and buckhorn bars
FXWG: 'Wide Glide'. An FXEF with wider and slightly extended front forks, bobbed rear fender and a flame design painted on the five-gallon petrol tanks that appeared in 1980
FXS: 74 cu. in Low Rider
FXB: FXS with black chrome and paint and both the primary and final drive were toothed belts
FXR, FXRS: five-speed versions of the FX Super-Glide fitted into a new frame
FXRT: touring version of the FXR
FXSB: FXS with the twin belts

1978   75th anniversary editions with commemorative paintwork produced across the range of models
1979   80 cu. in engine available in the Low Rider and Super-Glide and later on in the rest of the FX range. FXEF introduced
1981   the 74 cu. in engine was discontinued
1983   five-speed gearbox introduced on the new 80 cu. in FXR and FXRS

THE V2 EVOLUTION, 1984 to the present day

The development of the Harley-Davidson big twins since the Knucklehead has been one of slow and steady refinement over the years. The Panhead was the result of designing a new top end that was attached to the bottom half of the existing Knucklehead engine. In 1955 the bottom half of the Panhead was updated internally and this was used as the base when it was time to fit the Shovelhead's new barrels and heads.

In time the bottom end of the Shovelhead received an overhaul, and several years later this was used as the base for the new Evolution

Below **1990 FXSTS Springer Softail that reintroduced the Springer front forks last seen on a Harley-Davidson in 1948. The rear shock absorbers are tucked away underneath the frame lending a 'rigid' look to the frame.**

engine. The new engine has a direct ancestry that goes back to 1936, which provided the inspiration for the new model's name.

The V2 engine was one of two projects that were started in the period when the AMF corporation briefly took over the company, from 1969 to 1981. The other project, a water-cooled V-four engine is still sitting on a shelf in the factory, presumably alongside a previously halted V-four project from the 1920s. After some of the senior managers at Harley-Davidson had negotiated the buy-back from the parent AMF corporation in 1981, attention could be firmly focused on the introduction of the V2 Evolution. After 'Blockhead' failed to stick it became known as the 'Evo'. Earlier engines had cylinders made of cast iron, but for the first time the Evo was given alloy cylinders with iron linings and alloy heads that have been extensively worked to meet emission laws and burn lead-free fuel.

The big twins got the new 80 cu. in engine in late 1984, while the Sportsters had to wait for two years. They have come to be regarded as extremely reliable and worthy successors to a proud heritage.

FLT: basic model with modern fairing
FLHT: FLT with traditional handlebar fairing
FLHS: basic FLT with clear windscreen
FXR: basic Low Rider in the FLT rubber-mounted frame
FXST: update of the Wide Glide look in a frame with hidden rear suspension
FLST: FXST Softail with traditional cosmetic features
FXD: new rubber mount frame with a 'Dyna' exhaust system

Other model derivatives only have cosmetic differences.

V2 EVOLUTION SPORTSTER, 1986 to the present day

Although the Evolution Sportster had grown out of the Iron Sportster half of its engine's components are new and like the big twin, it has hydraulic valve lifters installed for simpler maintenance.

XLH: Sportster available as 883, 1100 and 1200 cc models

1985 FL and FXR received a five-speed gearbox and belt drive
1986 FXST received a five-speed gearbox
1988 85th anniversary models with commemorative paintwork offered
1991 Sportsters received a five-speed gearbox and belt drive

Left Evolution Sportster that has been fitted with a tank and seat made by the Storz company and a selection of performance parts. The whole package emulates the look of the successful XR-750 racer and XR 1000 road model, and gives back to the Sportster some of the performance that noise and emission laws have strangled over recent years.

CUSTOMS

CUSTOM

It was not long after peace was declared in 1945 that America found itself threatened again, but this time by an invasion from one of its former allies. Britain was rebuilding its economy after the devastation caused by the Second World War and was earning money from the export of its products all over the world. To assist the rejuvenation of the world's economy, the American government imposed very low import taxes on goods entering the country from abroad. The Ariels, Triumphs and Nortons that began to cross the Atlantic were 350 cc models at first, but these were soon followed by 500 and 650 cc bikes that were significantly lighter, cheaper and faster than their American rivals, although for sustained highway cruising at a relaxed pace there was still no substitute for a large V-twin. Not only were they taking sales away from Harley-Davidson, but they then had the audacity to win races too, Norton for example winning America's premier race, the Daytona 200, from 1947 to 1949.

Left **1975 FL Shovelhead that displays the lengths that owners have to go to, to get noticed in the dresser class at custom shows.**

Below **The jewel-encrusted white leather 'buddy' seat is the crowning glory on this sparkling 'dresser'.**

Above **Close-up of a Knucklehead engine that has been extensively chromed and gold plated.**

Another direction entirely was chosen by thrill-seeking Harley-Davidson riders. They wanted excitement with a rougher edge to it, and chose to differentiate themselves from the respectable dresser owners by 'bobbing' their bikes. This entailed removing all excess weight to make the bikes quicker and give them a mean and dangerous look. Off came the windscreen, saddle bags, crash bars, horn, primary chaincase, front mudguard and extra lights, while the rear mudguard was 'bobbed' by cutting off half of it. These bikes were purely functional, raw looks and performance were everything and the behaviour of many of the riders complemented their machines.

Above **West Coast styled Sportster. A look that was pioneered by Arlen Ness in the early 1970s.**

It is rather ironic that just when Harley-Davidson introduced the Panhead in 1948, regarded by many as the most beautiful and perfect example of the V-twin they had ever produced, that some riders began taking their bikes apart and throwing half of the bits away. Harley-Davidsons at the time were grossly overweight even without all the touring accessories that were considered necessary by many riders. A fully dressed 1200 cc 1952 Hydra-Glide weighed in at around 600 lb in comparison to the British 500 and 650 cc bikes that were under 400 lb and capable of similar performance.

It was here that Harley-Davidson owners split into two groups who went down different roads that would only really meet again forty years later.

The touring and club riders carried on as they always had before, loading up their bikes to go on sedate rides at the weekend with other like-minded riders.

The Hot Rod scene that paved the way for more decorative custom bikes was well established by the early 1960s in California. Just as the Hot Rods were based on what was being raced on the drag strips, so also did motor cycles look there for their styling inspiration. The bikes that raced had longer than standard front forks and a small skinny front wheel for improved handling in a straight line, yet their frames were built so that the machine still remained close to the ground. When many people started fitting long forks to their stock machines, the invariably standard frames caused the front of the bike to be lifted up. This was a cheap and simple way to make a stock bike look radically different but it also made it extremely unstable to ride. Cruising down the highway was fine on one of these but cornering took a great deal of concentration. In time the Knuckle and Panhead frames were raked at the front by angling the headstock out to bring them down to an even and lower level.

Above **Supercharged Shovelhead on the street at Sturgis. 'Performance is everything.'**

There were shops around then that had been catering for building and decorating the Hot Rods, and they had the facilities and experience to carry out elaborate paintwork, chroming and welding on these cars. These shops were increasingly utilized by people who wanted such work done on their motor cycles, and by the mid sixties ornately decorated choppers, and shops that catered exclusively for them, were well established in California.

Dennis Hopper was part of the scene back then and captured

Right **Parked outside the *Easyriders* magazine merchandise truck are reconstructions of the two Panhead choppers that were ridden by Dennis Hopper and Peter Fonda in *Easy Rider*, the film that was responsible for turning many of today's riders to Harley-Davidsons.**

Above **Arlen Ness riding through Deadwood, aboard the unfinished bike that he took to Sturgis in 1992. This was also the year in which he was inducted into the National Motorcycle Museum's Hall of Fame.**

boundaries of motor-cycle design that bit further. Each bike that he builds today still shows his preference for long, low, sleek machines and maintains his illustrious reputation. Twenty-five years after he first wielded a spray gun, he is still regarded by many as the greatest

the bikes and lifestyle in the film *Easy Rider* that went on to carry the style of these choppers all around the world.

It was 1968 when Arlen Ness first became involved in customizing. He had had to wait until he was thirty before he got his first motor cycle, an old Knucklehead. But once he had put it together and personalized it, his friends started coming round to ask him to perform similar work on their bikes. In time he opened a small shop and his reputation for innovative styling became legendary as each new custom that was wheeled out of his workshop pushed back the

Right **'Telesis', meaning the future progressively planned, was built by John Reed and won the prestigious ISCA national championship in 1990. Its 90-day conception to completion time scale is testament to the skill and teamwork involved in building a show winner. The subtle 'star' pattern, as seen on the rear disc cover, is echoed on the many hand-made components like the exhaust, hand grips, engine covers, risers, headlights, fork tubes, etc.**

Above **A spectacularly extreme example of a 1970s-styled chopper.**

Above **Looowww Rider. The closer to the ground a motor cycle is – the better it looks. Many customs achieve this by using spine-jarring rigid frames without shock absorbers, to enable the bike to hug the tarmac. This innovation chooses instead to lower the rider and still keep a degree of comfort with the luxury of rear suspension.**

artist in his craft. In recognition of his customizing work he was inducted into the Hall of Fame at the National Motorcycle Museum in Sturgis during the 1992 Bike Week.

John Reed is not alone in claiming Arlen Ness as his biggest inspiration, but he is very much his own man when it comes to creating his own work. Like Arlen, who designs parts for Drag Specialities, John works for Custom Chrome in a similar capacity and also creates extraordinary motor cycles.

By the 1970s the chopper style had come a long way from the chunky fat-bob look of twenty years before. The petrol tank had shrunk to a minuscule size, the king and queen seat had increasingly exaggerated proportions and the sissy bar and exhausts seemed to compete with each other to see which could be the tallest.

Harley-Davidson could not ignore this huge market for their used machines and eventually started producing their own new motor cycles that bore obvious influences from the custom scene, though in a very sanitized form. Their first model was the 1971 Super-Glide that blended the Electra-Glide and Sportster together to create a motor cycle that featured the best of what both had to offer. This was an instant success and by the end of the decade it had become available in several other versions, the Low Rider with slightly extended forks and the Fat Bob with large dual petrol tanks. All these bikes were based on the styles that the customizers had created and helped to sustain interest in Harley-Davidsons at a time when Japanese bikes were flooding into the country. The increasing popularity of these bikes resulted in the Wide Glide of 1980, which wholeheartedly embraced the customizing scene. This was basically a Fat Bob but with wide front forks, bobbed rear fender, forward controls on the highway pegs and flames painted on the tank – and was the first real 'Factory Custom'.

Karl Smith, or 'Big Daddy Rat' as he is more widely known, is a T-shirt salesman and creator of 'The Rat's Hole Custom and Chopper Show', which has been an annual fixture at Daytona since 1973. Not only is this one of the most prestigious events on the custom show circuit but it is also the first major competition of the year. Consequently it provides the earliest opportunity to view what people have been wrenching, restoring and customizing in their garages during the winter lay-off, and previews what will become the 'hot' new features and accessories on the street during the coming year.

There can be around 300 bikes competing for the top prize in each of the fifteen classes – from early antique models to exotic creations that will spend their brief life being carried from show to show. What is unique to the Rat's Hole Show is that the winning bikes and owners are flown across to Germany to be displayed at their motor-cycle trade show – the largest in Europe. Similar requests to view the winners have also come from other countries and in recent years there have been further trips to Sweden and France.

In the hope of enhancing the appeal of their bike to the judges

and bettering their chances of winning, some owners will dress in clothing that matches the design or colour of the paintwork and sit on their bike for hours. Others might arrange for a pretty girl to drape herself over the bike to attract photographers, and attention away from others in its class.

Encouraged by the success that the Daytona Rat's Hole Show enjoys, Big Daddy Rat now holds a second show at the Sturgis City Park during the Bike Week later on in the year.

Above **Close-up of a turbocharged Harley engine at a show, illustrating the quality of engineering and design that is necessary to be a contender for the top prizes.**

Right **Karl Smith with his entourage of 'Ratmates' and leering furry rodent pose for photographs at Daytona Beach in the mid 1970s.**

Above **Owned by Keith R. Ball of *Easyrider* magazine and built by Pat Kennedy in California. The right pedal controls all three disc brakes via a proportioning valve, while the left operates the clutch allowing the handlebars, with the internal throttle cable, to remain clean and uncluttered. The small hump on the left side of the handlebars is the rear view mirror!**

It is the small and innovative touches like this and the exhaust pipes, that are solid at the tip and have the exit hole for the gases a few inches along, that distinguish the show winners from the also rans.

Left **Performing for the photographers in a colour co-ordinated costume while the old man applies the final polishing touches prior to the judging at the Rat's Hole Show.**

While America is still where many of the major innovations in customizing come from, different countries around the world have formed their own distinctive customs that are suitable for their conditions and lifestyle.

Australia is a land with great contrasts in its climate. Distances between cities can be vast and the changes in conditions can be extreme. A rider can journey from a cool temperate area in the South East of the country to the subtropical and tropical regions in the north, crossing vast deserts in between. Right across the south of the country the endless Nullabor Plain stretches for thousands of kilometres, while a trip down to Tasmania off the south coast can subject the rider to icy blasts of wind and rain from the roaring forties, straight from the Antarctic.

The custom bikes that are ridden here have to cope with these

Above **Here is a twin-engined Harley with a difference. Instead of arranging them in line, the builder has mounted the two 61 cu. in Sportster engines side by side.**

roads and conditions and it is not unusual for them to clock up 15–25,000 kilometres a year travelling between the numerous parties and shows. Consequently there are few show bikes on the road and they are built more for practicality and comfort for the rider while covering long distances at speed. The roads that run between cities are sparsely populated and even the rider of a Harley with a five-gallon tank will often need to carry extra fuel to reach the next petrol station. Form follows function, and handling and high performance are more important than a superfluous decorative style. While the bikes are still highly individual, if a part is not practical or does not aid performance in some way it is usually left off.

Left **Murray from Victoria, Australia, aboard his 95 cu. in Harley that has a Softail style frame made from scratch in carbon steel and many parts worked from blocks of super hard aircraft aluminium. The engine may look fairly stock from the outside, but in the quest for high performance, many of the standard components have been substituted. Here the engine cases, pistons, barrels, heads, cam, ignition and carburettor are just some of the parts that have been replaced by others from performance accessory specialists like Sputhe, S & S and House of Horsepower.**

It is fortunate that Harley-Davidson are the only motor-cycle manufacturer who will still readily sell you an engine on its own. For without this option there would not only be far more piles of discarded and superfluous parts than there already are, but there would also be far fewer Swedish choppers riding through Scandinavia.

In a country which endures long dark winters and condemns riders to months of time to plan and build, it is not surprising that when the brief riding season in the sunshine does arrive, they want to make the most of it.

With so much time on their hands and well-equipped club houses to spend it in, they are prepared to put an incredible amount of effort into building something unique.

Typically most of these bikes are built around a new 80 cu. in. Evolution engine that is the only element of the bike purchased new from the Harley-Davidson catalogue. This is mated to an old Shovelhead four-speed gearbox, which enables a kick-start to be fitted, while a foot clutch/hand shift keep the handlebars clean and simple. Everything else is handmade in a style that is universally recognizable and unequalled anywhere else in the world.

Forks are – in a word – long. Twelve inches over stock length is widely regarded as the minimum, eighteen inches, getting there, twenty-four inches – perfect. Lights are functional, mudguards minimal if at all, front brake optional and an eighty-spoke front wheel compulsory.

Seating is as low as possible and a fat tyre and thin leather seat are all there is in the way of comfort for the rider on the rigid frame.

While the style is distinctive the features of the bikes are anything but similar. On the best examples there will barely be a part that, if not made from scratch, will not have been extensively reworked. On the best examples every single nut and bolt will be handmade.

The only element that largely remains untouched is the engine. High-performance engines are the exception rather than the rule and the only modification that is usually made is to put on a decent carburettor. The laws governing what you can ride on the road may be relaxed here, but speeding and other traffic offences are dealt with extremely harshly. As a result everybody adheres to the speed limit and absolutely nobody drinks and drives.

Above **Hand-built Swedish chopper with front forks 24 inches overstock that was built by Tommy 'Bempa' Grytegard, and which typifies the clean and uncluttered styling of the custom bikes in this country.**

Below **The world's longest Harley with front forks 236 inches overstock – Swedish of course. Despite the radical lines of many of the choppers in this country, the quality of engineering is such that the handling is often as good as, and sometimes better than, many stock bikes. This particular example, though, is a glorious exception to that rule.**

While Sweden has relaxed construction laws and strict speed limits, Germany has the exact opposite. Here there are the tightest construction laws in Europe, while on the autobahns there is no limit – in fact going too slow will get you stopped and fined.

The TUV laws that govern any vehicle modifications here mean that any significant part on your motor cycle that has been changed has to be approved first at a testing station, and again at an annual check.

Consequently most modifications go on inside the engine and Shovels and Pans are the preferred powerplant. Bored, stroked, open primary belt drive and if the rear drive was not by chain originally it would be converted to one, to allow the fitting of the fattest rear tyre possible.

Above **German Panhead that has been customized in a flat track style. While the newer Evolution engined motor cycles are difficult to modify and get through the strict TUV test, these older models have less of a problem. Although in this case the rider would have to make a few changes, like re-fitting the front mudguard, before he took it along to the testing station for its annual check-up.**

Right **The quality of much of the paintwork on the show bikes would be more at home on an art gallery wall.**

The first Harley-Davidsons imported into Japan were at the request of the Imperial Army in 1912 who ordered a small batch for some lucky soldiers. It is fairly certain that they remained in a stock condition – they never did order any spare parts!

They are still in demand today, despite the punitive taxes that are imposed on imported motor cycles, and there are over thirty dealerships in the country.

Most of the riders are content to keep their bikes' stock and just bolt on the factory-approved accessories. There are two distinct types of riders though, who are not content with riding stock bikes, but make subtle changes that will not offend in their society. Customizing is generally restricted to stripping down modern Electra-Glides to make them look like old Panheads with large buddy seats, trumpet-shaped horn and period paintwork.

The members of the Nagoya Harley-Davidson Club are an example of the Japanese desire to wear uniforms and conform even when they are not conforming. Attired as they all are in a police patrolman's leather jacket and boots with regulation whistle, baton and handcuffs hanging from their belts, their motor cycles complete the image for they are all fully dressed FLH Electra-Glides with flashing blue lights, CB radios and sirens to complement the 'Police' and 'Retired FBI Agent' stickers on their white fairings. Once a month they will meet for an orderly ride along the congested streets of the city and out through the paddy fields, keeping in strict formation, their progress cleared by two members riding two blocks ahead of the pack.

Below **When you are determined, nothing will keep you out of the wind.**

The mid-1980s brought an upsurge of interest in Harley-Davidsons after the introduction of the Evolution engine. Not only was it a match for reliability compared to other motor cycles but it still exuded the style, charm and looks of the bikes they had made fifty years before. The world economy was in a healthy state and nostalgia was what it used to be. Sales increased to a point where the media took note of this upsurge of interest, and as they appeared in more films and advertisements, so sales went up again.

Nowadays many of the new Harley riders dress and look like respectable versions of the riders of old, by whom society used to be so affronted. As well as the motor cyclists who changed brands, many more in their thirties and forties were enticed back into motor cycling by the chance to buy the motor cycle and dress like the person that their parents never allowed them to own or to be. Consequently the appearance of the many different people who ride today can be disarmingly similar.

The black leather, back patches, studs and tattoos may be found among the Harley Owners Group members almost as much as it will be among the outlaw clubs who have ridden Harley-Davidsons for years, and the custom bikes that they ride are generally less extreme in design than they used to be and are built more for good handling and increased performance.

Above **A selection of Harleys owned by members of the 'Hamsters'. Choppers with morbid and fantasy tank murals are becoming fewer and fewer in number on the streets today as riders build more bikes like these – with colourful paintwork and high performance engines.**

Below **To achieve a balanced overall design, the many components should complement each other. On this Hamster-owned bike even the handmade saddlebags echo the paint scheme.**

Below **Customizing is all about creating a motor cycle that is unique and says something about its owner. Here 'Junky Jim' makes his statement.**

85

Today several of the bikes in the Harley-Davidson range still echo the past in their styling and borrow back the ideas and alterations that customizers have brought to their motor cycles. The Softail in particular with its rigid-looking frame, huge tank, high bars, skinny front wheel, highway pegs and bobbed rear fender is not just an update of the 1980 Wide-Glide, but is a look that goes back another thirty years before that.

Above **The 'Heritage Royale' was inspired by the streamlined curves found on the very rare Bugatti Royales and the standards of craftsmanship that was lavished on them. Bob Dron decided to construct a motor cycle in a**

similar way to the coach builders of days gone by, who would take a car chassis and create the bodywork to a customer's requirements.

Starting with a Softail frame which was left stock he crafted by hand, the bodywork out of aluminium and the chrome strips from brass, while an Ostrich in Australia donated its hide for the seat. The finished motor cycle is valued at $125,000.

When it was entered at the Oakland Roadster Show it collected every motor-cycle award going and also walked off with the A1 Slonaker Memorial award, which is given to the most innovative new design in customizing – the first time that a motor cycle has ever won it.

CLUBS

Extract from a letter sent to the British Harley-Davidson club magazine – *The Harleyquin* – in 1952:
'It isn't until a chap, who has been used to a good spirit of comradeship, has to do without it that he realizes just how much it means to him. It was so with me, having been used to the great spirit of comradeship which existed in the old Indian Mountain Artillery in the 1920s. I quickly realized that here, in the Harley club, was the very spirit for which I had been looking. After my first club run I knew, more than ever, that by being a member of a Harley club I would gain everything and lose nothing.'

THE HAMSTERS

The Hamsters are a close-knit circle of around 125 friends spread all over America, many of them working in the motor-cycle trade as customizers and bike builders. What they all have in common is a love of Harley-Davidsons and the ability to build, or money to buy, some of the most innovative custom bikes seen in the shows or on the streets.

The origin of their name is explained by Arlen Ness: **'We are a bunch of friends who just like meeting up and riding together. One of the guys had a Hamster painted on his bike and it became something of a joke to refer to each other as Hamsters. Calling ourselves that emphasizes the fact that it is a lightweight social club and that we ride together for fun.'**

Left The Hamsters contain many of the best customizers in the world – like Arlen Ness, Dave Perewitz and Donnie Smith – who built this 'Shovelution'. Taking a 1979 Shovelhead and fitting Evolution barrels and heads to it before going on to hand-make most of the external parts.

Right The Hamsters commemorative T-shirt for their 1992 meeting at Sturgis, featuring a fifth face amongst the presidents on Mount Rushmore.

SEATTLE COSSACKS

'We are a fun team – doing a co-ordinated and skilful show-off show and if we can think of a stunt that might be done on a motor cycle, then we will bust our asses to try to make it happen.'

For over fifty years they have been delighting audiences by showing off up to thirty-five times a year and riding nothing but Harley-Davidsons.

Just like a ringmaster, Dave Eady captains the Seattle Cossacks as if he were running a circus. Controlling the crowds, clowns and gymnasts – not with the whip but a microphone.

With his carefully waxed moustache he looks every inch the showman, as one minute he deliberately gives the mischievous 'rookie' of the squad a hard time to play for the crowd's sympathy, and the next announces in a reverential tone that the sixty-seven-year-old veteran of the team will ride his bike while doing a headstand on the headlight.

The story of the Seattle Cossacks began in 1938, when some of the competitors at Seattle's 'Jolly Rogers Hill Climb' became bored during the long breaks between their runs up the near-vertical slope. To amuse themselves while waiting their turn they would perform tricks on their Harleys for the crowd. Before long the crowd began to take as much interest in the stunts as they were in the sport. So the riders clubbed together to buy a Harley-Davidson just for their trick riding. One thing led to another and before long they were putting on their own displays.

They chose to call themselves Cossacks,

the Russian word for the expert Ukrainian horsemen who were hired to protect Russia's borders, as this would reflect the skill with which they rode their motor cycles.

Today there are twenty of these 'horsemen' in the squad with varying degrees of experience – from Sam, the twenty-one-year-old 'Rookie' – to John Moser, who has spent forty-two of his sixty-seven years with the team.

The team has ridden on Harley-Davidsons exclusively and their bikes range from the oldest, a 1930s VL, through other 45, 74 and 80 cu. in side valves with a couple of Knuckleheads and a 'modern' 1950 Panhead.

These are all owned and maintained by each rider on the team, and are equipped to look original and as close to the style of the 1938 founding year as possible.

'The fact that we go out and party with each other and learn about each other means that we get to know and understand each other more than just on the motor cycles and knowing one's team members so well can only make the stunts better.

'We have never had a woman in the team though, in fact we have never had a woman even try to get into the team. Some of them ask but when we explain

to pursue coming into the team.'

While the members perform such difficult stunts, mishaps are bound to occur. Usually it is just a grazed knee or scratched footboard, although during the 'flower' once – the stunt where four men all balance on one bike and lean out in different directions with their heads grazing the ground – **'One of the men got a muscle spasm and could not come up again when the man on the other side did. With all the weight just on one side of the bike it was impossible to control and the whole bike toppled over, trapping John's boot in the chain and severing three toes.'**

Above A headstand by a Cossack, as old as his motor cycle.

Left Captain Dave Eady, on the left, leads his team on to the display ground.

Right The Cossacks performing 'the flower'.

to them what it's like out there . . . **Some of the situations that we get in, we have to get a hold and grab whatever we have to, to y'know hold on. And if you have to grab someone by the er. . . ear to hold on, then you're gonna do it and you hold on until the stunt is over. You couldn't just turn loose because it's 'Oh that's a girl'. No, if you're gonna fall off you would grab her to keep from falling off or dropping a stunt. We're not saying we don't want women in there, but when we start explaining what might happen – none of them have ever tried**

John Moser still continues to do some of the more dangerous stunts, though – like a headstand on the headlight while he is riding along or riding two bikes at the same time. **'We love to do this because of our love of motor cycles and to better the image of motor cycling. For example, I have had women in their eighties who have never ridden a motor cycle in their lives, come up to me after watching a show to ask me if I would give them their first ride . . . and I always say, "Yes ma'am, I sure will," and it's a thrill and a pleasure to do that for them.'**

THE TEL AVIV HARLEY-DAVIDSON CLUB

To most people who have not actually travelled in the Middle East, the holy land of Israel conjures up a picture of an arid and inhospitable land crossed by dusty trails. While there is desert and an average temperature of forty degrees in the shade – if you can find any – it is also a beautiful country that is blessed with forests, waterfalls and some superb highways.

The Israeli police force rode Panheads here from 1948 to 1956 and currently have ten FXRPs in their ranks. But it was only in 1989 that Harley-Davidsons came to be first officially imported into Israel. In the three years since then, seventy new Sportsters and two Low Riders have arrived to join the eight Panheads, three Shovelheads, two Servicars and one Knucklehead in the country.

With import taxes trebling what the bikes cost in America, it is not surprising that the people who can afford to buy them tend to have good jobs. Well-paid work or not, the owners still have to put much of their spare cash towards running and maintaining their Harleys. While the single dealership is importing new bikes, spare parts and accessories do not seem to be a priority. Fortunately the organizer of the club, Alon Avidar, has spent time in Los Angeles building Harleys, and has the contacts to order spares and the ability to help build and maintain his friends' motor cycles.

'We meet up to go riding in the desert, have parties, get drunk and do the same stupid things that Harley riders do in Sturgis.' 'We ride because it is our way of life and because it gives us the key to perfect freedom. There is nothing above a Harley-Davidson, except the blue sky and pure heavenly satisfaction.'

THE HARLEY OWNERS GROUP

There are two reasons why Harley-Davidson is a thriving company today. One is the Evolution engine that has achieved a perfect blend of old design and modern reliability, and the other is the Harley Owners Group. Many of the people who are now purchasing Harley-Davidsons are switching from other makes or returning to motor cycling after a number of years away. To sustain the interest of these new owners, generate friendship and better the image of motor cycling, HOG was created by the factory in 1983. Membership now exceeds 150,000 people and is divided into 600 chapters worldwide. Each chapter is sponsored by the local dealer and the whole organization is in the charge of Bill Davidson, great-grandson of one of the company's four founders.

Since 1990 they have expanded into Europe, beginning with Great Britain, where the first European rally was held, and subsequently spreading throughout the continent leading to the two most recent HOG groups that were formed in Switzerland during 1992. While they sell only 500 of their motor cycles there every year, the country has more Harley-Davidsons per capita than anywhere else in the world.

Harley-Davidson has adopted the Muscular Dystrophy Association as its chosen charity and together with the HOG groups has raised over $12 million to date. This is a continuous fund that is swollen by local events as well as at the large rallies held all over the world. If you can enjoy yourself, better the image of motor cycling and raise money for a deserving charity at the same time, then everyone benefits.

Right Long time HOG member.

Left The Tel Aviv H-D Club against the ancient wall of Jerusalem.

THE VIETNAM VETERANS MOTORCYCLE CLUB

The Vietnam Veterans Motorcycle Club was originally formed as a riding brotherhood for survivors of the conflict, but it also embraces veterans from the Second World War, Korea and the Desert Storm Operation. The requirements for membership are simple: to have served your country and to ride an American motor cycle. It is not just a motorcycle club but also a network of support, and a tireless campaigner for justice and the rights of its members who have only in recent years achieved the respect and gratitude of many of their fellow countrymen.

Rolling Thunder – the annual ride to the Vietnam memorial wall in Washington, DC – is the major run of the year for these veterans, their families and their many supporters.

Its aim is to pay tribute to and remember those who gave their lives in the wars that have kept their country free. It also publicizes the fact that there were many others who went 'Missing in Action' and that there is a widely held belief that 'Prisoners of War' still remain against their will in Vietnam.

Rolling Thunder V, in 1992, brought 60,000 riders into the nation's capital to honour their comrades and to add pressure to the riders' demands that the MIA/POW situation be fully investigated.

Left Paintwork detail on a Vietnam Veteran's Harley.

Right Until recently, the only motor cycle available to a Czech rider who wanted a Harley-Davidson would be one of the old WLAs that were left behind after the Second World War. Enterprising Czechs would dress them up to look like Electra-Glides.

HARLEY-DAVIDSON CLUB, BRNO, CZECHOSLOVAKIA

The Brno Harley-Davidson Club may not be the largest or oldest of the two Harley-Davidson clubs in Czechoslovakia, but it is certainly the most dedicated. The Prague Club, founded in 1928, is the oldest Harley-Davidson club in Europe; although it merged with a vintage car club to enable it quietly to survive the years of oppressive communist rule. Club Brno, though, refused to disband or hide under another name, and as a consequence its members endured many hardships. For the crime of publicly demonstrating a liking for the United States and their 'decadent' products, the members of the club were registered by the secret police and subjected to constant harassment and arrests. They were not allowed to travel out of the country and always passed over for promotion at work – even their children were refused places at university.

The country used to be a thriving export market, for Indian and Excelsior as well as Harley-Davidson, all of whom had dealerships there in the 1920s and 30s. The rise of fascism and the Second World War ended all foreign imports to the country, and apart from the sale of some ex-Army WLA bikes between 1945 and 1947 there have been no new motor cycles officially imported for nearly sixty years.

The Brno Harley-Davidson Club was formed by six friends in 1963 to pool their knowledge and resources and keep their motor cycles running. As there were no new parts available, everything that broke had to be made from scratch and whoever owned a Harley-Davidson had to be very skilled mechanically to keep it on the road. Despite all the difficulties, by the late 1980s the club had grown to forty members.

Shortly after the 'velvet revolution' had cast out the old communist government, the Brno Harley-Davidson Club was able to host its country's first international rally in 1990.

Not untypical of the dedication of its club members is Radovan Podskalsky, who many years ago discovered the remains of an old F-head engine along with a few other bits and pieces. In time he managed to collect some pictures of what the whole bike looked like and armed only with the knowledge of the size of the original wheels plus a lot of skill and intuition, measured the other parts in the pictures and worked out their dimensions. Seven years later after making from scratch a frame, pistons, wheels, brakes, bearings and many other components, he was finally on the road.

NORMAN (THE BOOZEFIGHTER)

If you have ever seen the film *The Wild One* then you will have seen Hollywood's version of what happened when The Boozefighters and the POBOBs (the 'Pissed Off Bastards Of Bloomington') rode into the sleepy town of Hollister in 1947.

At the end of the Second World War returning servicemen were eligible for the 52/20 veterans' benefit. For a year they were able to receive $20 a week from the state while they looked for work. After they were demobbed in California, many of them settled there and spent their severance pay on a Harley-Davidson and their weekly allowance on petrol and beer. Sometimes they would ride in large groups to small towns that were holding country fairs or race meetings. Once there they would party for the weekend in a manner that was described as boisterous or riotous depending on whose account you read after the event.

The 4 July weekend in Hollister was the destination for one of these runs. Different sides tell different stories about what actually

happened there, but the outcome was that the local police called in the state highway patrol to try to restore order to the streets and the national newspapers picked up on the story and called it a riot in sensationalist prose on its front pages. For many years after this event the media depicted Harley-Davidson owners as lawless rebels who travelled in large gangs ravaging everything in their path.

In 1983 a reunion was organised for the original members of the Boozefighters, all now in their fifties and sixties, yet many of them still riding.

'We had one rule that said you had to be "Boozefighters Up" at all times. If you passed out, you'd better land on your face, 'cause if you landed on your back and covered up that Boozefighters insignia you were out of the club. We used to tell each other, "Keep an eye on me. If I crash on my ass, roll me over quick before a club officer sees me."

'We did things like fall out of windows and set buildings on fire, but we did them in innocence. When a member would fall asleep at a campground or something, we'd pour a circle of gas around him and his bike and light it. That woke him up fast. But we never tried to hurt anybody, because we had all been hurt in the war. Believe me baby, all of us had suffered in that war.'

In 1948 several members of the POBOBs formed the first chapter of a new club in San Bernardino: the Hell's Angels. Norman has been a Boozefighter since 1956. **'Nowadays we party with all the clubs – Bandidos, Hell's Angels, Sons of Silence and get along with everyone. In fact we are probably the only club that gets along with everyone.'**

Left Boozefighters back patch.

Right Norman, sergeant-at-arms for the Boozefighters.

THE CHRISTIAN BIKERS

'Anywhere that motor cyclists gather you can be sure to find some of our members among them, because we love bikes, bikers and Jesus.'

The Christian Motorcyclists Association, with 35,000 members, are the largest of innumerable groups of Jesus bikers riding Harleys for the Lord. While the Wheels for Jesus, Tribe of Judah and Sons of God are among many others trying to gather up the rest of the flock.

On the Main Street of each major event in the motor-cycling calendar in every American state, the CMA will be raising funds for their 'motor cycles for missionaries' programme and dispensing the word of God or handing out free cups of iced water bearing 'facts about heaven and hell'.

Cheryl Cilenti: **'My husband and I used to belong to an outlaw motor-cycle club, but my heart now desires to tell them of the Gospel of Jesus. I was an** addict to marijuana for over eight years, an alcoholic and user of crack and speed. I used to pack guns, but now I pack the word of God, the Bible.

'We must use our Harley-Davidsons as tools and nothing more, for we have only one God.'

Below left The CMA dispensing warm vibes and cool water at a race meeting.

Below Happy couple who are 100 per cent for Jesus.

THE HARLEY-DAVIDSON RIDERS CLUB OF GREAT BRITAIN

It was the year that Honda made their first motor cycle that a group of friends first discussed the possibility of a national Harley-Davidson club in Britain. There were very few pre-war Harleys still surviving in the country but the government were offloading many WLAs that were surplus to requirements in peacetime and at reasonable prices too. When the club was officially formed in 1949 there were thirty members all mounted on WLAs but in time a few Model Js and Vs were turning up at the club nights. The London dealer Fredrick James Warr (established in 1924 and still London's only Harley-Davidson dealer) specialized in British motor cycles at the time but, encouraged by his son Fred H. Warr, became more associated with Harleys – buying up surplus bikes and converting them into civilian trim.

Fred H. was one of the early club presidents and the workshop was where committee meetings were held, and when everything else was moved out, club dances. At one point it even had a licensed bar installed.

In the 1950s Fred H. Warr opened the first post-war shop in the country that catered exclusively for Harleys and in subsequent years invited the members to build a clubhouse on the land beside his country cottage – The V-twin Saloon – where many a run ended.

It was not until 1957 that any new bikes from Milwaukee were allowed to be imported, and the few that trickled in were beyond most people's pockets after astronomical import tariffs. WLAs were still the mounts of most of the club members and breakfast runs to the South Coast and camping weekends were the most popular events.

The club began venturing into Europe to meet other enthusiasts in the 1960s and were instrumental in creating the Federation of European Harley-Davidson clubs and the European Super Rally that is still the largest annual Harley gathering in Europe. A far cry from the days when a meeting of 150 was regarded as 'an awesome spectacle'.

In the early 1970s the availability of new bikes increased and prices came down to a more affordable level. This attracted a new and younger element into the club, inspired by the films and magazines that were coming across from America, and events became more numerous and broader in appeal to cater for everyone. Today the members' ages range from twenty to seventy and the club remains Great Britain's premier Harley-Davidson club. As their name infers, they are a riders' club – no trailering to events.

Above Ken 'Scottie' Myers, President of the Harley-Davidson Riders Club of Great Britain. Serving with the USAF in England, he is the first American to be elected to this position.

THE CAPITALIST TOOLS MOTOR-CYCLE CLUB

Above Members of the Capitalist Tools lined up behind a 1965 Panhead Electra-Glide.

Right One of Malcolm Forbes unique hot-air balloons takes off.

In 1965 an employee of the late Malcolm Forbes came to him for a loan to buy a Harley-Davidson. Although Malcolm considered motor cycling to be dangerous, he lent him the money on condition that he could see the machine after it was purchased. The story goes that when the employee returned to show him the new Electra-Glide and offered him a go, he rode away and did not stop riding until the following morning. Whereupon the forty-five-year-old immediately went and bought one for himself. He later went on to gather a large collection of vintage Harley-Davidsons and always had

one stationed and ready to roll in all his houses around the world. If he was away from home then he would simply carry one of his machines on his private jet or yacht.

'The Capitalist Tools' were created by Forbes as a riding club for him and his Harley-riding employees. The name comes from a dismissive remark made by the Russian premier who met Forbes when he was riding through their country. To the premier, who referred to the Harley-Davidson as a Capitalist Toy, Forbes replied: 'No, they are Capitalist Tools.'

Ballooning was his second greatest passion

and the Capitalist Tools would also take to the air with him. He still would not leave his Harley behind, though, for he commissioned an inflatable to be stitched in the shape of a huge Heritage Softail.

Either alone or with his club he rode through nearly every American state, ventured into the Arctic circle and across the Sinai desert and still found time to visit most of the interesting and unusual places in between.

'Sure, motor cycling can be dangerous, just like life can be dangerous – but life will certainly kill you.'

THE HELLAS HARLEY-DAVIDSON CLUB OF ATHENS

'It's no problem to leave your Harley unlocked here – they never get stolen.'

While they were only formed in 1990 many of the Hellas Club have been riding together for years, and own over fifty motor cycles among their thirty-six members. To comply with the law of the country, the club has to register with the police to be able to ride in a group, though this is merely a formality. For while the police are now compelled to ride Hondas, many of the older ones can fondly remember the days when they, too, rode Harley-Davidsons when on duty. Like most motor-cycle policemen around the world, they love to see the bikes and turn a deaf ear to the sound of loud exhaust pipes. But unlike most policemen, they also turn a blind eye to the absence of crash helmets on the club members' heads.

Below The Athens H-D Club line up beneath the ancient Acropolis.

THE COFFIN CHEATERS OF AUSTRALIA

The Coffin Cheaters are based in Perth, Australia, and are one of the largest clubs in the area, putting on some of the best bike shows and events on the West Coast.

There are a lot of outlaw clubs in this country and they generally get along together. If they do not, then they keep well away from each other, and don't turn up at events where they would not be welcome.

A confrontation between two clubs a few years ago ended with nine members killed, and generated the sort of publicity that affected all motor cyclists. The result was that everyone had to mature a lot and strive to regain the good will that had been lost. For it was obvious that situations like this would not only harm the members but the whole lifestyle would ultimately suffer too. Thankfully the situation today has become a lot more laid back, and big events like Aratula, Darwin River Rock and Ponde can attract dozens of clubs and thousands of people, yet still remain trouble free.

Right Club member from the Coffin Cheaters of Perth.

THE MOTOR MAIDS OF AMERICA

In the pre-war days many of the women who rode their own motor cycles were wives of men who owned dealerships. One such woman was Dot Robinson, daughter of the man who founded Goulding Sidecars and wife of Earl Robinson. Earl was a Harley-Davidson dealer and keen competitor in long-distance racing, at one time holding the cross-country record. His enthusiasm for the sport rubbed off on Dot for she also began competing in endurance events and twenty-four-hour marathons. She would invariably trounce the opposition in the ladies' races, and at times, earn a top-five placing when up against the men. When a friend of hers, Linda Dugeau, suggested that they should form a social club with their other female friends in 1940, the Motor Maids of America were born.

Men also benefited from the formation of the organization. For many women would only suffer their husbands going off on their motor cycles for so long before putting pressure on the men to sell them. Now that their wives could ride the bike and belong to their own club, the men could relax a bit more every time they said they were going out to meet their friends for a ride. The Motor Maids were keen to promote a positive side of motor cycling and vetted prospective members to ensure that they had

a spotless reputation before they could be considered for membership.

Their first and most important rule, which still holds today, is that each woman should own and ride her own motor cycle. Expulsion is the penalty for any woman who trailers her motor cycle to an event.

Their 600 members still wear their uniform at meetings and parades – grey slacks, white boots and gloves, tie and bright blue shirt. Rider safety is very much part of their image and crash helmets are worn. Bare heads, shorts and abbreviated costume are not permitted.

At the age of eighty-one, Dot Robinson still rides a Harley-Davidson, a 1990 Heritage Softail, and in her fifty-three years with the club has never missed a convention.

Right A selection of pictures of the Robinson family taken in the 1950s. The bottom picture features Dot aboard a 1945 Knucklehead and her daughter Betty in their Motor Maids uniforms. In some years Dot would ride 50,000 miles travelling on club business and has covered well over a million miles on her 35 new Harley-Davidsons between 1928 and 1990.

THE HARLEY-DAVIDSON CLUB OF SWEDEN

The highly organized and efficient way in which this club is run is typified by the price of insurance that their members now pay for their motor cycles. For the club lobbied the insurance companies and persuaded them that Harley owners rode in a more responsible manner and were in fewer accidents than owners of most other makes. The result is that they now pay significantly less for cover than the owners of Japanese motor cycles. The club produces a book listing the names and addresses of all of its 3500 members so that anyone who breaks down can look up their nearest member for assistance. What would be used as a thieves' reference book in many other countries is not abused here. Theft of Harley-Davidsons in Sweden is rare. For not only will riders refuse to purchase stolen parts, but their bikes are so individual and handmade that the components taken off a stolen bike would be too easily identifiable. This is a country where every self-respecting Harley rider builds his bike from the ground up and it is not unusual for even the most minor components to be worked from solid metal.

Below Anders Johansson and his rigid Shovelhead. When he runs out of rallies and parties and the bad weather comes round in Sweden, he simply ships his bike to America or Australia or wherever and just keeps on riding.

RIDERS

Above There were few women motor cyclists back in 1967 when Jo Giovannoni learnt to ride on a kickstart and hand shift Panhead, and for many years she rode alone or in the company of male friends. In the early 1980s this situation changed as more women took to riding their own Harleys and she founded the second chapter of the all-female club 'Women in the Wind'.

Like her, many other women were desperate for a publication about Harleys that was not also a 'skin' book, and that reflected their interests. So, she started her own magazine. Seven years later *Harley-Women* still caters for these riders and after twenty-five years and eight motor cycles, she can still vividly remember the memory of that first ride on the Panhead.

RAY AND SELMA

'The best trips are the long runs, when it becomes an automatic reaction to wake up in the morning and get on the bike. All responsibilities vanish as a sense of freedom takes over and everything else ceases to exist. It's just you and your partner out in the elements amidst the sights, sounds and smells of your environment. Isolated from each other yet sharing the same experience.

'The Harley breathes and vibrates like a real motor cycle should. You can feel that it was designed and made by people and that it is not just a piece of technology that a computer has decided is a solution for transport.

'Riding a Harley instils in us a sense of belonging to the tradition of the open road. Wherever we stop the people we meet can recognize this and friendships can be formed that instantly cross any barrier of language or race.

'Many people think that we are fools for exposing ourselves to discomfort and possible risk while riding. Well, we hope that we don't get to know any better. We only have to take a look at our neighbours stagnating over a weekend to make us want to go out for a ride. If we can still be riding together in our eighties, then our life will have been a happy one.'

Right Ray and Selma – sharing the same experience.

WERNER TRIELOFF

'I was fifteen years old and living next door to the County Police Station in Ober-Allgau, Bavaria, when I saw my first Harley-Davidson. It was 1945, just as the war ended, and two to three times every day the American Military Police would routinely call in at the Police Station on their snow-white Harley-Davidsons. Everything about them fascinated me – the sound of the engines, the relaxed style in which they rode – the whole image. The thought of possessing such a machine seized hold of me, and this infatuation has never left.

'It was another eighteen years before I could finally own one – a Hydra-Glide which I bought in 1963. This was followed by a Duo-Glide and in 1974 a brand new Electra-Glide. I have owned this ever since and it is the motor cycle that I want to be with until I cannot ride any longer.

'I almost lost it in 1987 when my sixteen-year-old son, Bjorn, wanted to have a go on it. When he turned on the petrol the carburettor overflowed, and as the engine started the whole bike was engulfed in flames. I was not able to get the fire extinguisher off the bike in time, but an alert neighbour was quick to act and together we managed to put it out, fortunately before the petrol tank could explode. My son and I stood together for a long time afterwards, broken, looking at the burnt remains. The next day we started to take it apart and we began restoring it together.

Above Werner Trieloff in evening dress at the Club Brno rally dinner in Czechoslovakia.

'I do not take part in many national events in Germany, preferring to travel to other countries. Probably the most memorable of all my experiences took place while on one of these trips. I rode across to England for the European Super Rally in 1979 with four friends. There was a petrol shortage and rationing was in force, everyone was limited to buying one gallon at a time, if, that is, you could find a petrol station open. Fifty miles after my last fill up I was the first to run out. As fuel was so precious it was doubtful whether anyone else could or would stop to help. My motor cycle is fully equipped with blue lights, fire extinguishers and a siren and I ride wearing a policeman's leather jacket, jodhpurs and knee-length black boots. When a passing policeman in his patrol car stopped to see what the problem was, he spoke to me in a comradely way as though I was a member of the German police force. Upon hearing that my tank was dry and believing that I was an officer of the law, he stepped out into the road and stopped a large van that was passing. Producing a hose he ordered the surprised driver to siphon out some petrol for me and then called up another police car to escort us to the nearest petrol station to lead us to the front of a very long queue. We parted in great friendship and this experience of friendship between nations was an amazingly positive influence on me that I often look back on with fondness.

'Harley-Davidsons are simply a philosophy. You ride one and you have an indescribable feeling of assurity and joy in the knowledge that you are on the king of the road.

'I always feel at one with the world whenever I begin a new ride; that is how it is for me and I am glad it is so.'

MARLA AND SKOOTER

'Skooter's the third dog that has ridden with me. He just came up to my bike one day and would not go away. So I said, "Look, this is me, this is my motor cycle and this is life on the road"; he looked us over and still stayed put, so I told him to hop on.

'I used to travel to bike events every weekend and would invariably bump into the editor of *Supercycle* at most of them. He eventually suggested that as I was there I should take some pictures and write about it for the magazine. So I did – and pretty soon afterwards, I packed up my job and rode away to do it full time. That was five years, five Harleys and a quarter of a million miles back. Now I only come home every three months for a brief break.'

It's a familiar sight at American events to see Marla and Skooter turn up on her 'decker' – 'it's Canadian terminology and I'm still Canadian.' Together they ride all over America, making all of the big events and most of the smaller ones too. While they are away they send back stories about what's happening, when and where, which are printed in her 'Prowlin' the Parties' pages in *Supercycle*.

'I don't get attached to my Harleys at all and never wash them. Once they hit 50,000 and the one-year warranty expires I buy a new one and hit the road again.

'Cats! I hate 'em.'

Right Marla and Skooter loaded up for the next trip.

ZOLTAN SULKOWSKY AND GYULA BARTHA

Above The secondhand side-car outfit that carried Zoltan and Gyula around the world, decorated with their collection of badges from the motor cycle clubs that they encountered on the way.

In 1928 Harley-Davidsons were sold in over a hundred countries around the world. One of these countries was Hungary, where two twenty-five-year-olds decided to see the world and chose a Harley-Davidson side-car outfit as the ideal form of transport.

They bought a used 61 cu. in. model J with a side-car, stuffed $600 in their pockets and left Budapest in August to travel west across Europe to Portugal. This was quite straightforward as the roads were good and the people they encountered were friendly, but this all changed after they had sailed across to North Africa. Here there were no roads, only rough and rocky camel trails, and the people they encountered were anything but amiable. They passed through the heat and dust of Morocco, the Sahara desert, Libya and Egypt without too many problems but after entering Palestine their good luck ran out when they were attacked on the road that led to Damascus from Nazareth. Here armed Syrian Bedouin on horseback chased them, while the two men returned fire and clung on for dear life. Despite the rough track they were riding on they kept the throttle wound open and fought the machine as it bucked and threatened to overturn for twenty minutes until they had managed to outrun their pursuers.

Shaken, they escaped into Turkey until they risked travelling south again, down through Sudan and on to a boat that took them over the Arabian Sea to India.

While they were there, they completed a 600-mile tour of the country and sent articles to magazines around the world to finance the next part of the trip, before hitching a lift on a freighter bound for Australia. Upon arriving at the port they discovered that their magazine articles had made them famous and there were hundreds of people there to greet them. After briefly enjoying their new celebrity status they left Freemantle and rode around the perimeter of Australia and visited Tasmania, clocking up another 7000 miles in the process. After hitching another lift on a boat leaving Brisbane they went island hopping and rode through Java, Sumatra and Borneo before tackling the jungles in Cambodia, Laos and Vietnam.

It was in 1930, two years after leaving home, that they crossed yet another border and entered a Chinese village. Almost immediately they were held up by gunmen who took everything except their papers, petrol cans and, thankfully, their Harley. Nothing was going to stop them now though, and they managed to continue through China and Korea where another boat was found to transport them for a brief stop in Japan and then across the Pacific Ocean to Hawaii. From here it was just a short hop to California and Hollywood. The film studios had learned of their epic trip and brought out their stars like Greta Garbo and

Charlie Chaplin to be photographed on the motor cycle. These pictures were seen all over America and the publicity generated meant that they were recognized throughout the country and could raise more money on their travels by giving talks to the towns they visited. Their celebrity status was not going to slow them up though and they continued riding throughout America and Canada until they turned up at their home from home, Milwaukee, Wisconsin. Here the Harley-Davidson factory welcomed them, and their outfit was overhauled and tidied up in preparation for the most arduous part of their journey through South America. After Mexico and Cuba it took two years to reach Rio de Janeiro, via Colombia, Ecuador, Peru, Chile, Argentina and Brazil. While they had become experts at traversing seemingly impossible landscapes on narrow tracks, here there was

only jungle and impassable rivers. Sometimes they could only manage eight miles a day and they frequently had to employ Indians to carry the dismantled machine over mountains or use canoes to float the parts across rivers.

It was once they had arrived in Rio that they decided it was time to return home and a passage was booked to England. On their final ride through the city they were accompanied to the port by the local police force – all mounted on Harley-Davidsons – for a grand send-off. After crossing Europe for the second time they arrived back in Budapest in July 1936. They had taken eight years to travel 110,000 miles through sixty-eight countries. **'We only wanted to undertake this trip on a Harley-Davidson and we could only have completed it on a Harley-Davidson.'**

PAUL KOMAR

'I am President of the Turul Harley-Davidson Club in Hungary and my life and love is the Harley-Davidson motor cycle.

'I saved for years to get my first Harley – an ex-Army WLA that was in a hundred rusty pieces. It took two years to make the parts that were missing, clean and repair what I had, and assemble it all together. After it was completed I sold it and all of the possessions I had and travelled to Germany. When I returned I had spent all that I owned in the world on a totally broken 1987 1100 cc Sportster. I was so happy – for to own a Sportster has been a dream for all of my life, even if it did take another one and a half years to complete its repair and get it on the road.

'Now I can ride free in a country that is free again.'

Above Paul Komar and the last of his old parts that were sold to finance his Sportster.

'FRENCHIE'

'I ain't gonna tell ya how I got my name but it goes back to my wilder days riding with "The Outlaws" out of New Jersey and later on The Breed.'

Like many long-time Harley riders in America today Frenchie has a past, not all of it he is particularly proud about – **'but hell, it was fun at the time.'**

'I've been riding Harleys since the early sixties and am now on my 27th – a 1977 Low Rider, and as long as I have the strength to climb on and kick-start it I will always ride American iron. When I can no longer do that – well, life will not be worth living. For many years I was a tattooist travelling from party to party – most days I could make $300 yet by morning it would have all been spent on getting high and buying a few parts for my bike or on getting me out of jail.

'Eventually it all became a hassle – the constant harassment by the police, getting into trouble, going to prison. When the drugs became a need rather than a desire I thought – "Hey, wait a minute – this isn't me," and I quit them. A lot of my friends from my early days didn't make it, though, and are dead through dope or bike accidents.'

Today Frenchie is a highly skilled toolmaker and lives in Akron, Ohio, and the only fighting he indulges in is for preserving the freedom that Americans have always cherished.

'Crash helmets suck – period. If people want to wear them believing they are safer than going bare-headed, fine. But when you are sliding down the street and that helmet catches something, then it will break your neck

every time. California has just been forced to pass a compulsory helmet law and it looks like every state is now going to fall. This is something we have to fight all the way to the Supreme Court. When the government tells you to do something it is impinging on your freedom and this country is based on the freedom of the individual.

'I would never ride a Japanese motor cycle. Our fathers fought against the Japs and they have not forgiven us. They flood our market with their motor cycles and all but prohibit our motor cycles from entering their country.

'I ride a Harley-Davidson because it's American-made and because it's an American tradition. If I was born a hundred years ago I would be doing this on a horse.'

Left Frenchie, proud to ride American.

Right Chris Carr of the Harley-Davidson racing team. Winner of the 1992 Camel Pro Championship. The same year he also won his fifth consecutive 600cc series National Championship.

PAM CUMMINGS

'I have always kinda liked to go fast and believe that it comes from my family's genes, for all of my four brothers have raced cars on the dragstrip. At the age of twenty I suddenly decided that I wanted a motor cycle even though I had never ridden one, and three months later after passing my test I was the proud owner of a 1978 Sportster. One day my husband, John, wanted to see how fast his 88 cu. in. Panhead would run so he took it to the Great Lakes Dragaway at Union Grove in Wisconsin. While I loved to ride fast on the expressway, I told John that there was no way that I would ever take my motor cycle up a dragstrip – but the following year I had a try-out on a 1982 Low Rider that I had just bought to replace my Sportster and was bitten by the drag-racing bug.

'With practice my times got faster and in the winter of 1986 we stroked the engine to 96 cu. in, and I began racing during the 1987 season in grudge matches at Union Grove and got my times down to around 11.5 seconds.

'John then decided to build a drag bike for me because I was constantly breaking my street bike on the strip, only to want to ride it to work the next day.

'The next step was to build a bike to race in the 'Modified FL' class. This is a class for stock 80 cu. in Harley-Davidsons with modifications for drag racing, such as head work, carburettor, exhaust pipes and so on. When we campaigned it nationally in the 1989 season with the American Motorcycle Racing Association (AMRA), we succeeded in taking the number two national position in the class and briefly held the quarter-mile class record. The next two years also brought number two in the class and it was starting to get boring to ride – I needed a change. A friend of ours let me try his Fuel (nitromethane) racer out for size in the pits, and once I got on and blipped the throttle, I knew this would be my next challenge. I decided that I would be the first female Harley-Davidson Fuel pilot in the United States. We call ourselves pilots because at the speeds we run at you are really piloting the machine, not riding it.

'Pro Fuel is the class for an unlimited cubic inch Harley-Davidson running on nitromethane, direct drive, high gear only – which means that you can attain tremendous speeds of over 150 m.p.h. in the quarter mile.

'We built this awesome machine over the winter and completed it by mid 1992. With its 80 cu. in engine stroked to 99 cu. in and wheelie bars it spans almost fourteen feet. I have been taking my time in building up the speeds, but at each of the AMRA races I went to in '92 I qualified. My best time so far in the Eighth Mile is 5.90 seconds at 128 m.p.h. Later in the season, though, I broke my ankle racing in West Virginia and that has put me out for the rest of the year – but I'll be back.

'The competition is serious, but the support and camaraderie between the racers is matched by no other.'

Right Pam Cummings takes off at the Clarksville Harley nationals in 1992.

Above Perry on the driveway in front of his house.

LORD PEREGRINE ELIOT – THE EARL OF ST GERMANS

The sign at the entrance to the Port Eliot estate in Cornwall is the first indication that 'Perry' is not a typical peer of the realm and member of the English aristocracy. 'Take extreme care, children and motor cycles are everywhere' it says.

'**Peer comes from the Latin word *par* which means equal. I am among my peer group in the House of Lords and I am among my peer group when riding with others on Harley-Davidsons – we're all equals.**

'**I vividly recall the early 1960s when** we would ride flat out and six abreast down the dual carriageway to Southend with the police sirens on our bikes blaring out. This was back in the days before helmets were compulsory and was a genuine one-per-center experience – a hooligan, mad max, thundering high – WOW!**

'**I can also painfully recall pushing my WL 750 nine miles into Rome while it was fully laden for touring two up. My companion had a twisted foot from a previous spill in the Swiss Alps – so I** had to do all of the pushing. It was a Sunday afternoon on an August public holiday and 90 degrees in the shade. All of the returning drivers without exception blasted their horns as they slowly crept past me in a vast slow-moving traffic jam. I get a headache even to recall that ghastly day.'**

Perry is an honorary vice-president of 'The Harley-Davidson Riders Club of Great Britain' and for twenty years has invited its members to his idyllic stately home for an annual weekend. '**You ride a Harley-Davidson with style and dignity because you are proud to ride a motor cycle that has no rival.'**

WILLIE G. DAVIDSON

'Willie G.' is the grandson of one of the company's four founders and was around Harley-Davidsons even before he could walk. In his capacity as Vice-President of the design department he is given much of the credit for the styling of Harley-Davidson's first modern bike – the 1971 Super-Glide, and for most of the innovative designs that followed, like the Café Racer, Wide-Glide, Low Rider and Heritage Softail.

'While the image has changed over the years it will always be ride to live – live to ride. What Harley-Davidsons offer is a sense of freedom and

Below Willie G. and Nancy Davidson at a European HOG rally in France.

adventure which goes beyond what other motor cycles offer and because we have gone through evolutionary rather than revolutionary changes we have never forgotten where we have come from.'

Harley-Davidson is the only motor-cycle manufacturer that has a policy of not endorsing the compulsory wearing of crash helmets, although they do recommend that one is worn. This is backed up by Willie G.'s personal opinion.

'Riders should be free to choose whether or not they wish to wear crash helmets. It makes me uneasy to think that this freedom of choice can be taken away. Education about how people should drive their cars and ride

their motor cycles is the best option.'

Indeed every one of Harley-Davidson's motor-cycle executives has successfully completed a Motor-cycle Safety Foundation course.

Willie G. attends Harley Owners Group rallies and events all over the world to meet the people who ride his company's products. He is always available to any rider who wishes to speak to him, take a picture or request an autograph – and it is no exaggeration to say that you will never hear a bad word said about him.

Nancy and Willie G. have three children who now also work for Harley-Davidson and continue the family link with the three Davidson brothers who began it all in 1903. Bill is the worldwide head of HOG, Karen works on the styling of the Motorclothes and William J. manages the Events and Entertainments Marketing.

KEITH R. BALL

Keith R. Ball has been the editor of *Easyriders* magazine off and on for the last ten years. Since the magazine first appeared in 1971 it has devoted its editorial content solely to Harley-Davidsons, particularly customized ones, and has been a forthright campaigner against compulsory helmet laws and other unjust and discriminatory legislation. Even when Harley-Davidson went through a

difficult phase in the seventies, it has remained the lone voice in the motor-cycle press to stick by the company. As Keith rightly claims, **'*Easyriders* has gone a long way to help build this industry and actually kept Harley-Davidson going through the tougher times.**

'What were my best and worst experiences aboard a Harley-

Davidson? Well, I can tell you about my best memories – they usually involve girls . . .

'**Actually one of the best experiences was the Liberty Run to Washington that I attended in 1992 along with 50,000 other motor cyclists. It was an event put on by the motor-cycle rights groups in and around Wisconsin, which brought all the riders together to make a statement to the government, as to how strong these guys feel about motor cycling – how unified they are and how they are devoted to keeping it free.'**

What Keith is too modest to mention is that he was once the national director of ABATE (A Brotherhood Against Totalitarian Enactments), the principal organizers behind this rally and one of the largest motor-cyclist pressure groups in America, and that prior to the Liberty Run setting off for the state capital he was invited to address the crowd. One of the placards on the run accurately summed up the riders' message to the politicians: 'I work, I ride, I vote – Be very scared of me.'

'**I've only ever had one accident, and I've never collided with a car. I've fallen down plenty of times – but then that's just part of the game.**

'**I won't ride anything but a Harley-Davidson. Anytime I want to clear my head or if I have a negative thing going on in my life – something that's disturbing me, like a bad relationship or even a bad day at work – getting out and going for a ride always clears my mind and makes me feel whole again.'**

Today *Easyriders* magazine sells 350,000 copies a month and is the biggest-selling motor-cycle magazine in the world. '**But we are just a bunch of guys who have been riders ever since we were sixteen. We really love what we are doing and we try to portray that on the pages of the magazine.'**

ROD GLUE

Inherent in the Australian character is the larrikin, rebel and renegade, sprinkled with a dry sense of humour.

This originated in the early colonial days over two hundred years ago, when the first convicts arrived from England to serve their sentences. The prisoners had to be tough and resilient individuals to survive the brutal regime in the gaols, where the gaolers were often no better than the criminals.

Prisoners who had served their sentences and free settlers gradually started to swell the fledgling colony's population, and exploration of the vast unknown continent began.

The infamous bushranger, horseman and big thorn in the side of the bureaucrats was Ned Kelly, born of Irish parents in Australia, not far from where Rod Glue lives in North-Eastern Victoria. For years the elusive Ned was a rebellious and popular challenge to the empire's planned status quo, the authoritarian rule from afar and the oppression it stood for. They hanged him, aged 26.

In the 1850s, substantial gold discoveries brought a second big wave of migrants to the still new colony of Australia with another reign of brutal oppression from the administrators, police and politicians. This erupted in the miners' revolt against the police with the fierce stand-off at Eureka Stockade and a win for the miners' rights, after loss of life.

This resentment of authority, antagonism towards the privileged classes, shared camaraderie in difficult circumstances and individualism have left their mark in the development of the Australian character.

These traits are still apparent today, and the Australian Harley riders fit neatly into the picture.

Rod lives in Victoria and works as a freelance photo-journalist for Australian and international motor-cycle magazines.

Right Rod Glue enduring the drudgery of going to work – riding out on another tough assignment to report on a rally.

JOHN REED – CUSTOM MOTOR-CYCLE BUILDER

'I have spent most of my nearly fifty years learning about motor cycles and doing my best to turn my ideas into reality. I am still an apprentice, and feel more frustrated now than when I first started and thought I knew everything.

The older I get the less I know. I am very serious about it, and spend eighteen hours most days releasing my dreams from their metallic prisons. I am extremely difficult to work with if my team mates do not put in as much effort as I do.

'I am not motivated by money, and have had to make a lot of sacrifices to be in a position to see a few of the ideas that torment me come to fruition.'

John started 'Uncle Bunt's Chop Shop' in England in the early 1970s.

'The custom scene was crazy at the start and there were only a few of us involved, but it gradually got really commercialized. A lot of career capitalists came in and it became far too serious. I felt I was needed at the

Left and right John Reed and the Albino Sturgis that he was commissioned to build by its owner, who wanted something special to ride to the 50th Sturgis Motor Classic in 1990.

start because there was a lot of aggravation – mostly from the traditional motor-cycle press. At the start I did not even like choppers, but one of my weaknesses is to fight for the underdog, and I fought like a son of a bitch. When the chopper/custom scene stabilized I moved on to my true love, which is building bikes.'

In the early 1980s he moved to California to work for one of the largest manufacturers of custom parts and accessories for Harley-Davidsons.

'I am now employed at Custom Chrome designing parts, and taking mine, and other people's ideas from conception through production-quality prototypes to a production package. I personally process an average of thirty-five new products a year but I try to limit this to a respectable time to enable me to invest the rest of my energy building personal projects which I almost never sell.

'My reason for working in a large corporation is to take a very expensive prototype which could only be bought by the rich, who don't usually deserve it, and mass produce it, so it can enter the true custom competition. The ultimate and true competition is when a person goes into a retail store, looks over a range of parts, picks yours over everyone else's and likes it enough to hand over his money for it. Especially if instead of paying several thousand dollars for a handmade one-off, he is actually getting a better part at a realistic price. My career ambition is to design and produce a part which would be willingly bought by every motor cyclist in the world.'

Left 'Bear' on his 1970 Electra-Glide which is still in its original blue and white paint. When he is not riding, he works as an actor – playing 'the biker' in TV commercials and movies. 'Although I mostly end up on the cutting room floor.'

Right This backpiece may only be skin deep, but the commitment to Harley-Davidsons goes a lot deeper.

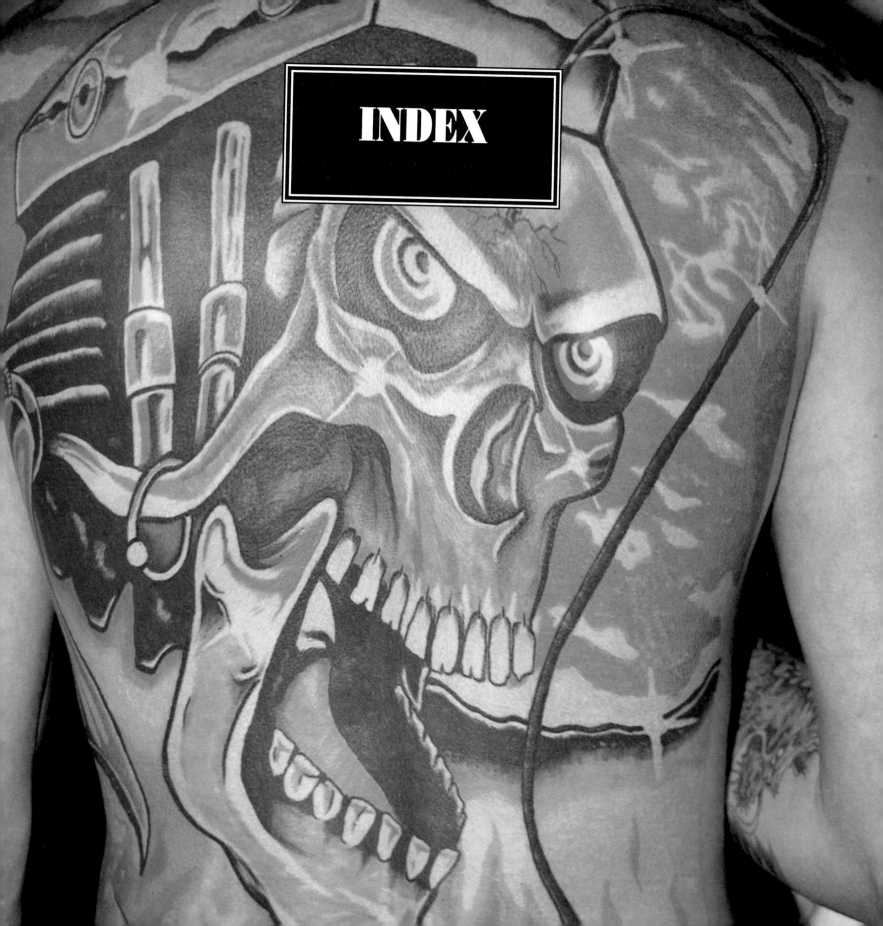

ACKNOWLEDGEMENTS

Martin Norris would like to thank all of the people who appear in the Riders and Clubs chapters for allowing me to feature them, and in most cases, for their friendship.

The following people deserve a special mention, either for their contributions to this book or for their contributions to my life on the road.

Reed Resnikoff of Hong Kong HOG; Robert 'The mad Swede' Lofgren; Paul Komar in Hungary; Radovan Podskalsky and The Brno Harley-Davidson Club in Czechoslovakia; Eric Miclot, Rosie Peroz, Niglo Harley-Davidson Club; Harley-Davidson Frontiers Club in France; Werner Trieloff, The Bones MC in Germany; HOG Switzerland; Alon Avidar and the Tel Aviv Harley-Davidson Club; The Harley-Davidson Club of Poland; The Harley-Davidson Club Indonesia; Yoshimi Sugimoto of Harley-Davidson Japan; Rod Glue, The Harley-Davidson Club in Australia; Rick and Kay Chamberlin; The Jackpine Gypsies; Dave Eady and the Seattle Cossacks; John Reed; Big Daddy Rat; Willie G. Davidson; Dot Robinson; Jo Giovannoni of *Harley Women* Magazine; Keith R. Ball of *Easyriders* Magazine in America; and Ken Lee, Tony James, Ian Mutch, Steve Berry, Perry Eliot, Trudi and George Waller, Ray and Selma Hurst, Stefanie Foster, The Sussex Coasters, The Harley-Davidson Riders Club of Great Britain.

All photographs by Martin Norris with the exception of the following: p100 (above and right) Classic American; p36, 37, 80 (left), 103 (right) Rod Glue; p39, 81 (above and below), 106 Robert 'The Mad Swede' Lofgren; p92, 102 Ian Mutch. Boozefighter quotes on p97 courtesy of *Easyriders* magazine.

First published 1993 by Sidgwick & Jackson Limited

a division of Pan Macmillan Publishers Limited
Cavaye Place London SW10 9PG
and Basingstoke

Associated companies throughout the world

ISBN 0 283 06164 2

Copyright © Martin Norris 1993

The right of Martin Norris to be identified as the
author of this work has been asserted by him in accordance
with the Copyright, Designs and Patents Act 1988.

1 3 5 7 9 8 6 4 2

A CIP catalogue record for this book is available from
the British Library

Photoset by Parker Typesetting Service, Leicester
Printed and bound in Great Britain by
BPCC Hazell Books Ltd
Member of BPCC Ltd